LOUISIANA
SCOUNDRELS

LOUISIANA
SCOUNDRELS

KILLERS, CULTISTS & THE UTTERLY DISSOLUTE

DR. ALAN N. BROWN

THE
History
PRESS

Published by The History Press
Charleston, SC
www.historypress.com

First published 2025

Manufactured in the United States

ISBN 9781467159029

Library of Congress Control Number: 2024944896

CONTENTS

INTRODUCTION

For many people, Louisiana is a world unto itself, completely different from the rest of the country, and in a sense, it is. Louisiana is best described as a melting pot of French Canadian, African and French culture. The state's contributions to American music and cuisine are easily recognizable. Some of the state's inhabitants—the Creoles and Cajuns—even speak a different dialect. Louisiana's bayous and indigenous species—especially the alligators—also set it apart. Louisiana's premier party town—New Orleans—is rivaled only by Las Vegas.

The darker side of a number of these individuals emerged because of their professions. The pirate Jean Lafitte is noteworthy because of his immensely profitable smuggling operation and the assistance he lent Andrew Jackson during the Battle of New Orleans. Eugene Bunch started out as a schoolteacher and politician, but he morphed into the "Gentleman Train Robber" to finance his gambling habit. Bricktop, a ravishing red-headed sex worker, was brutalized by her profession, but she found release in brutalizing some of her customers. The same can be said of Toni Jo Henry, the only woman to die in Louisiana's electric chair.

Several other Louisiana women turned to murder for different reasons. Antoinette Frank, a New Orleans police officer "gone wrong," shot and killed several workers at an Asian restaurant at the urging of her boyfriend. Clementine Barnabet is believed to have killed her victims with an axe as part of a voodoo ritual. Anne Plue Gartes, the "Louisiana Black Widow," is believed to have committed murder for the oldest reason of them all: money.

Then there are the serial killers who shot and stabbed their victims for no apparent reason. Mark James Robert Essex vented his hatred for white people by shooting several random people from the roof of a hotel. Russell Ellwood, the killer taxi driver, was driven to kill drug-addicted sex workers for some unknown reason. The Axeman of New Orleans, who was never caught, murdered and mutilated a number of men and women before finally disappearing.

The most baffling of all are the scoundrels whose victims were people they loved. One of the standouts is Dr. Etienne De Champs, who murdered a twelve-year-old girl whom he professed to love. Similarly, Zack Bowen stabbed and cannibalized his girlfriend during the aftermath of Hurricane Katrina. In his case, he was probably suffering from PTSD as a result of his miliary service.

Hopefully, as you read these bloody stories, you will not develop negative feelings toward the people of Louisiana. The state is populated with human beings who, like everyone on the planet, sometimes commit heinous acts of violence. Keep in mind that Louisiana is also made up of good, law-abiding people who put their lives on the line to bring the Louisiana Scoundrels to justice.

JEAN LAFITTE

THE TERROR OF THE GULF

In the eighteenth century, one of the means through which Britain extended its empire in the New World was state-sponsored piracy. The British partnered with pirates to plunder French, Dutch and Spanish ships to eliminate competition for commercial interests in the colonies. Many pirates viewed the ports of colonial cities, such as Boston, Richmond and Charleston, as refuges where they could entertain themselves when they were not scouring the high seas for vessels loaded with booty. Some of these brigands even conducted business with the governors of the colonies. One of these corrupt governors was Benjamin Fletcher, who was a business partner of Thomas Tew, the "Rhode Island Pirate." However, British attitudes toward piracy changed after 1713, when the empire condemned piratical activity in the colonies. The worst of these scalawags was Captain Edward Teach, more commonly known as "Blackbeard," who instilled fear in the hearts of colonists and sailors alike. By the time of the Revolutionary War, these enemies of the state were under control for the most part. Ironically, the Continental Congress made contractual agreements with pirates to seize and destroy British ships in the Loyalist regions along the coast. By the end of the Revolutionary War, privateers had seized more than $18 million in cargo from British ships. One of the most romanticized of these privateers who "worked for America" was Jean Lafitte, whose reputation vacillated between that of a gold-seeking pirate and smuggler and defender of New Orleans in the War of 1812.

Edward Teach, better known as Blackbeard, plundered merchant vessels in the West Indies and the American colonies until a small group of sailors killed him on November 22, 1722, just off Oracoke Island. *Wikimedia Commons.*

The details of Jean Lafitte's early life are sketchy best. He was probably born in 1776 to merchant-class parents in the Bordeaux region of France. His father was a smuggler named Pierre Lafitte. Jean's half-brother, Pierre, was the product of his father's second marriage. Jean went to sea at age thirteen. His prowess as a sailor earned him a promotion to the rank of mate on a French merchant ship that sailed around the Cape of Good Hope to India. A heated argument erupted between Jean and the captain. As a result, Jean left the ship at Mauritius Island. He did not remain unemployed for very long, because a gang of pirates who had anchored at the island were looking for new crew members. According to one version of Jean's early escapades, Jean soon became captain of the ship, which waged a number of raids against British ships much larger than his.

By 1800, the Gulf of Mexico was infested with pirate ships, which operated with impunity under international law when they flew the flag of the Republic of Cartagena, a seaport in Colombia. These privateers were supposed to target Spanish ships, but many of them preyed on the ships of other countries as well. Following the Louisiana Purchase, many pirates and privateers smuggled their ill-gotten gains into New Orleans, which was much closer than Cartagena. The base of operations for many pirates, like Jean Lafitte, was the Bay of Barataria, about sixty miles south of New Orleans. Pirate ships slipped through the narrow passage between the islands Grand Terre and Grand Isle. From their swampy hideout on Grand Terre, pirates and privateers supplied the merchants of New Orleans with a variety of goods at very reasonable prices.

Top: The Jean Lafitte National Park was named for the pirate's smuggling operations. *Wikimedia Commons*.

Bottom: Barataria Preserve outside of Marrero encompasses twenty-six thousand acres of bayous, swamps and marsh. *Wikimedia Commons*.

Until Jean Lafitte arrived in Grand Terre in 1810, fights between competing smugglers were commonplace. Lafitte established order on the island by uniting the warring factions. Before long, the inhabitants of Grand Terre called Lafitte "boss." He erected huge warehouses for the pirates' plunder and built cottages for their families. Lafitte also constructed quarters for the enslaved people he and the other pirates had stolen. The enslaved became "smuggled goods" after the United States ended the slave trade in 1807. Before the secret auctions that were held on the island, the enslaved were kept in pens or barracoons. The enslaved, who were purchased for $20 in Africa, were sold for between $800 and $1,000 to plantation owners in Louisiana.

Aided by his brother Pierre, Jean Lafitte now commanded a fleet of ten ships. With a crew consisting of Norwegians, Creoles, Seminoles, Frenchmen and Cajuns, Jean and Pierre plundered British, Spanish and American merchant ships. Around this time, Jean Lafitte and his brother opened operations in New Orleans's French Quarter. Most of the goods they smuggled into the city were taken from Spanish ships. According to legend, Lafitte's blacksmith shop was the base for the brothers' smuggling operation in New Orleans. Essentially, the forge and anvils served as a front for their smuggling activities. He was now more of a pirate manager than an actual pirate. When he was on shore, he socialized with naval officers, politicians and community leaders. He became well known for his lavish parties and cultivated manners. At this time in his life, Lafitte was a very romantic figure. Tall and handsome, he became a favorite among Louisiana's aristocratic women. In Lafitte's social circles, he was known as "Gentleman Lafitte," a name that distinguished him from his more introverted brother.

By 1813, Jean Lafitte had become the primary supplier of all the merchandise sold in stores in New Orleans. Governor W.C.C. Claiborne posted proclamations in public places in the city offering a $500 reward for the arrest and delivery of Jean Lafitte to the sheriff of Orleans Parish. Lafitte retaliated by posting his own proclamation throughout New Orleans offering a $1,500 reward for the arrest of Governor Claiborne

Lafitte's Blacksmith Shop is said to have been a front for the Lafitte brothers' smuggling operation from 1772 to 1791. *Wikimedia Commons.*

and his delivery to Grand Terre. Furious, Governor Claiborne arranged for a grand jury to issue indictments against Jean Lafitte, his brother Pierre and all the pirates and privateers of Bataria Bay on the charge of piracy. Claiborne also had Pierre arrested and jailed. Jean paid two of New Orleans's finest lawyers, John R. Grymes and Edward Livingston, $20,000 to defend his brother. Nevertheless, Pierre remained in jail for several weeks until he finally escaped during a jailbreak. Lafitte told his lawyers that in order to receive payment, they would have to collect it in person at Grand Terre. Livingston refused, but Grymes traveled to Grand Terre to get paid. The free-and-easy lifestyle of the pirates appealed to him, so he remained on the island until he gambled away all of his earnings—in three days—and then returned to New Orleans.

Governor Claiborne was not finished with Jean and Pierre Lafitte. His complaints to the federal government that Lafitte's unchecked smuggling was cutting into customs revenue prompted an attack on Grand Terre. On September 13, 1814, Commodore Daniel Patterson's ship, the USS *Carolina*, accompanied by six gunboats, took the pirates at Barataria completely off-guard. At the end of a brief battle, Patterson's forces captured nine ships, twenty cannons, approximately one hundred prisoners and $500,000 worth of goods. The Lafitte brothers and several hundred of their men escaped in the surrounding bayous.

Jean and Pierre headed straight for New Orleans, where Jean decided to prove his patriotic fervor, despite the destruction of his stronghold by Patterson's forces. A few days before the battle, Jean had met with British officers in Barataria Bay. They offered him a captaincy in the British navy and $30,000 in gold if he agreed to side with the British in an attack on New Orleans. Jean told them that he would consider their offer. Shortly afterward, he sent a report of the meeting to Governor Claiborne. Jean added that he would fight with Andrew Jackson's defenders of the city in exchange for a full pardon. On December 1, 1814, Claiborne then met with a group of miliary officers, including General Andrew Jackson, and informed them that he believed that Lafitte's offer was genuine, but Lafitte's offer was rejected. Unknown to Jackson, New Orleans had only one thousand "green" troops and two ships. The defenders also had the ships they had confiscated at Grand Terre but no sailors. Once Jackson had inspected the city's defenses and realized how weak they really were, he reconsidered Lafitte's offer. Therefore, when Lafitte met with the general a second time, the former pirate was told that Jackson would gladly accept his assistance in defending New Orleans.

Jean Lafitte was also given his own command, organized into military units known as the Baratarians. Lafitte's forces were armed with sixteen cannons. Lafitte suggested that the Americans' defensive line be extended to a nearby swamp, and Jackson agreed. On December 23, 1814, Andrew Jackson's forces attacked the British army, led by General Pakenham and his numerically superior force. The British forces advanced on the American lines on December 28, but an artillery crew manned by two of Lafitte's former lieutenants, Renato Beluche and Dominique Youx, repulsed them. The Battle of New Orleans ended on January 8, 1815. General Jackson recommended that Lafitte and one thousand men be granted a full pardon. President James Madison granted his request on February 6, 1815.

Two years after receiving their pardon, Lafitte and his men returned to their life of piracy. Some historians believe that Lafitte was still seething over the loss of his property that was confiscated after Patterson's attack on his old base at Bayou Barataria. People who were present at the great victory ball that was given on January 23, 1815, believe that Lafitte was angry because he had been snubbed by Generals Coffee and de Flaugeac. Even though the generals apologized to Lafitte afterward, he left the party convinced that, in the minds of many people, he would always be "Lafitte the pirate." Before returning to his old life of crime, Lafitte arranged for one of his financial backers to attend the general auction and buy back his ships that had been taken by Patterson's forces at Grand Terre.

In 1817, Lafitte and his one thousand crew members began attacking Spanish merchant ships. For their new base, Lafitte and Pierre chose Campeche, an island that is now known as Galveston, Texas. Within a year, the colony had between one hundred to two hundred men and women who lived in new houses they built themselves. As time passed, the size of the colony grew to over two thousand inhabitants and 120 buildings. However, many of the colony's men were criminals and fugitives from different regions, making it difficult for Lafitte to create an orderly community like the one on Grand Terre. The island's annual income was over $2 million, the source of which was mostly plunder taken from ships using forged letters of marque. For several years, Lafitte lived on the island in a grand mansion he had built for himself and his mistress, a free woman of color named Catherine (Catiche). The couple had two children, Marie and Jean Pierre. The colony's headquarters was a large red building that the pirates dubbed Maison Rouge. In 1819, Lafitte purchased a schooner that he christened *Bravo*. He ordered two of his lieutenants and a crew of sixteen men to sail the ship to Campeche, which was then known as "Galvez-town." On the way back to

This print by Currier and Ives depicts the Battle of New Orleans, which was fought on January 8, 1815. *Wikimedia Commons*.

their home base, Lafitte's men decided to attack a Spanish merchant vessel, even though the ship did not carry a privateer's commission. While they were looting the ship, they were intercepted by the American revenue cutter *Alabama*. Lafitte's men were tried, convicted and sentenced to be hanged. Through the use of clever legal maneuvering, Lafitte was able to get the men reprieved, but after the reprieve expired, they were all hanged as pirates.

Lafitte's difficulties escalated over the next couple of years. In 1820, a pirate known only as "Brown" attacked and looted an American ship in Matagorda Bay. The authorities traced the ship back to Galvez-town. Lafitte tried to appease them by hanging Brown in the harbor, but they decided that Galvez-town had to be destroyed anyway. Lafitte was given three months to dismantle his settlement and leave. After burning Galvez-town to the ground, Lafitte was said to have boarded the *Pride* and left on May 7, 1821, with large hordes of gold, his mistress and his children.

Lafitte's final years are as mysterious as his early years were. It is believed that Lafitte and his men continued taking Spanish ships in the Gulf of Mexico before establishing a base on the coast of Cuba. However, Lafitte and his men incurred the wrath of Cuban officials after attacking and looting merchant vessels carrying supplies to Cuba, so he sailed to Great Columbia, which was commissioning former privateers for its new navy. In June 1822, he was granted a schooner, the *General Santander*, and was legally authorized to take Spanish vessels. In early February 1823, Lafitte attacked what appeared to be two Spanish merchant ships in the Gulf of Honduras. Suddenly, they turned around and fired their guns at the *General Santander*. It turned out that they were actually warships of some sort. Lafitte was badly wounded and died on February 5, 1823. He was buried at sea. Thus ended the life of a man who insisted that he was a smuggler and a privateer, not a pirate. Many historians, however, remember him as the last great pirate.

As is true with the stories of many legendary figures, Jean Lafitte's did not end with his death. The most persistent of the Lafitte legends concerns the hiding place(s) of his gold. Possible hiding places are believed by many to be located in Galveston, Contraband Bayou in Lake Charles and Grand Isle. Legend has it that a swamp in Springfield, Louisiana, was drained because of the treasure that was said to have been deposited there. Gold is also believed to be in the remains of one of his ships that sank to the bottom of the ocean. Searchers still pick up loose coins around Barataria Bay.

An even stranger footnote to Jean Lafitte's life turned up in the 1940s, when John Andrechyne Lafitte began passing around a journal that had been written by his great-grandfather Jean Lafitte. The man claimed that he found the journal in a trunk he had inherited from his grandfather Jules. According to the journal, Jean Lafitte changed his name to John Laflin before returning to the United States. He ended up in St. Louis, where he married Emma Hortense Mortimer and fathered two children. Laflin died in Alton, Illinois, on May 5, 1854. One of the primary problems with Laflin's journal is the complete absence of marriage certificates or death certificates for John Laflin. In addition, his name does not appear on the tax rolls from any of the places where he supposedly lived. Despite the lack of evidence supporting the writer's claims, the "journal" remains controversial to this day.

A Lafitte legend that is more credible is set in North Carolina. The story goes that in 1823, Lafitte faked his death and relocated to Lincolnton, North Carolina, under the name Lorenzo Ferrer. In their book *Jean Laffite Revisited*, authors Ashley Oliphant and Beth Yarbrough provide initial support for the legend by proving that Lorenzo Ferrer was a real person whose name appears in the Hedrick's Company tax roll in Lincoln County, North Carolina. They also found Ferrer's name in a book called *Lincoln County Heritage 1997*, where his name appears as that of a guest at a hunting lodge with his beautiful octaroon mistress. Once Ferrer arrived in Lincolnton, he set about making himself a part of the community by joining a church, paying taxes, attending public events and joining the Freemasons lodge.

In the next decade, his name appears on the 1840 census. According to public records, Ferrer added enslaved people to his household in the 1840s. Records also show that Ferrer participated in Independence Day celebrations in 1847 and 1848. In the 1850s, Ferrer continued to buy and sell property, including an enslaved man named Ephraim. In 1958, he

This is a poster for Cecil B. DeMille's 1938 movie *The Buccaneer*, which focuses on the pirate's role during the Battle of New Orleans. The star of the movie was Frederic March. *Wikimedia Commons.*

supported the Democratic candidate for president and mourned the death of his octaroon mistress. During the Civil War, something that might have linked Ferrer to Lafitte was his concern that his chest of jewels and gold coins might fall into the hands of Yankee troops.

Jean Lafitte's influence has transcended the boundaries of legend and extended into the realm of literature. Lord Byron's epic poem *The Corsair* (1814) is based on the exploits of Jean Lafitte. In 1930, New Orleans author Lyle Saxon wrote the novel *Lafitte the Pirate* (1930). In Ruby Lorraine's children's story "Victor and the Pirate: A Story of New Orleans During the War of 1812" (1947), there is a fictional child who persuades Jean Lafitte to assist in the defense of New Orleans. In the second volume of Alvin Schwartz's *Scary Stories to Tell in the Dark* (1984), Jean Lafitte's ghost ship—the *Pride*—is sighted by a Confederate blockade runner. Jean Lafitte makes the acquaintance of the Time Commandos in Simon Hawke's science fiction novel *The Nautilus Sanction* (1984). Jean Lafitte's ghost tries to enlist the aid of a beautiful stripper in digging up his buried treasure in Poppy Z. Brite's short story "The Sixth Sentinel" (1991). Jean Lafitte appears in Isabel Allende's novel *Zorro* (2005). Author Aya Katz made Jean Lafitte a character in *Theodosia and the Pirates: The Battle Against Britain* (2013) and *Theodosia and the Pirates: The War Against Spain* (2014). Jean Lafitte is lost in the Bermuda Triangle in the science fiction novel *Atlantic Pyramid* (2014). Jean Lafitte and his pirate colony Campeche are important plot elements in Michael Punke's novel *The Revenant* (2002).

Early on, Jean Lafitte's adventures also proved to be ideally suited to the cinema. Cecil B. DeMille's 1938 movie *The Buccaneer*, starring Frederic

March, is based on Lyle Saxon's novel by the same name. Directed by Lew Anders, *The Last of the Buccaneers* (1950) stars Paul Henreid. A remake of *The Buccaneer* was released in 1958. The film was directed by Anthony Quinn, and it starred Yul Brynner as Jean Lafitte and Charlton Heston as Andrew Jackson. The Pier 21 Theater in Galveston shows an eighteen-minute film directed by C. Grant Mitchell year-round; the title of the film is *The Pirate Island of Jean Lafitte* (1998).

DELPHINE LALAURIE

NEW ORLEANS'S SADISTIC SOCIALITE

Marie Delphine McCarty was born in New Orleans in 1780 to affluent parents who had moved to Louisiana when it was still under Spanish control. Delphine was married three times. Her first husband was a high-ranking Spanish officer named Don Ramon de Lopez y Angulo. She and her husband had stopped in Havana on their way to Madrid when he died suddenly. She gave birth to their daughter a few days later. Delphine's second husband was a wealthy French banker, legislator and lawyer named Jean Blanque. They had four children before his death in 1816. Her last husband was a much younger doctor named Leonard Louis Nicolas Lalaurie. She and Dr. Lalaurie had two daughters together. In 1831, Delphine purchased a neoclassical mansion at the intersection of Royal and Governor Nicholls Streets. Because her husband was not present much of the time, the day-to-day management of the house and family was in her hands. She furnished the two-story mansion with wrought iron balustrades and beautiful chandeliers. Delphine soon established herself as one of the city's premier hostesses, treating her guests to fine food and champagne.

Despite Delphine's efforts to project the image of having a happy household, she obtained a legal separation from her husband in 1832, claiming that he had "treated her in such a manner as to render their living together unsupportable." Her own daughter from Jean Blanque supported her mother's claims. By April 1834, Delphine had returned to the house at 1140 Royal Street.

For many years, Delphine Lalaurie's house at 1140 Royal Street was referred to as the "Haunted House." *Wikimedia Commons.*

It turned out that marital strife was not the only secret Delphine was keeping hidden behind closed doors. In 1828, three years before Delphine and her family moved into their mansion, she was investigated for cruelty toward the people she enslaved, in violation of a local ordinance prohibiting the mistreatment of enslaved people. Court records indicate that Delphine hired a lawyer to plead her case and that she sold several of her enslaved people. By 1832, rumors of Delphine's abuse of her servants had escalated. Eventually, a court-appointed lawyer was dispatched to the Lalaurie House to see if Delphine's treatment of the people she enslaved had improved since 1828. One of her neighbors told the lawyer that Delphine chased an enslaved ten-year-old girl with a whip across the roof of the house until the girl tripped and plummeted to her death below. People said that Delphine punished the child for not brushing her hair properly. To avoid bringing negative attention to the Lalaurie family, Delphine buried the girl, Lia, on the property instead of in a slave cemetery. As a result of the lawyer's findings, Delphine was ordered to sell off nine of her enslaved people.

Another rumor that was making the rounds in New Orleans concerned the family's cook, who was supposedly chained to the stove. This seemingly apocryphal tale was substantiated one day in 1834, when the Lalauries' kitchen caught fire. The neighbors immediately notified the police and fire departments. When the first responders arrived at the Lalaurie House, they cautiously made their way into the kitchen. They were amazed to find the seventy-year-old cook chained to the stove by the ankle. The cook explained that she was so afraid of being punished by the Lalauries that she set the fire in an attempt to kill herself. While the men were unlocking her chain, she added that the enslaved people who were taken to the uppermost room of the house were never seen again.

Neighbors who had gathered around the front of the Lalaurie House attempted to break into the property's slave quarters to see if the enslaved had escaped the flames, but they were prevented from doing so by Delphine and her husband, who had returned home by this time. Several of the bystanders were so angry at being denied access to the slave quarters that they broke in anyway. The horrible sight that was spread out before them haunted their dreams for the next several months. One of the neighbors who was interviewed by a reporter for the *New Orleans Bee* was quoted as saying that apparently seven of the enslaved who had been imprisoned there for several months "were suspended by the neck with their limbs stretched and torn." Several of the bystanders who had forced their way into the slave quarters claimed they saw lacerations on the backs of some of the enslaved, who appeared to have been starved. The horribly mutilated bodies of the enslaved were said to have been found in the attic. One of the eyewitnesses, Judge Jean Francois Canonge, observed that an elderly enslaved woman with a deep cut on her head could barely walk. Another was wearing a spiked collar. Canonge said that when he tried to discuss the carnage with Delphine's husband, he was told to "mind his own business." Before long, the *New Orleans Bee* reported that after the sheriff dispersed the crowd of over four thousand, there was not much left of the home except for a couple of walls. The angry crowd had turned into an angry mob, destroying everything in sight, even setting fire to the house itself. Firefighters took the surviving enslaved people to the Cabildo, where hundreds of spectators stared in shock at their gaping wounds. Amid all the confusion, Delphine and her husband were able to make a hasty escape in their carriage. According to legend, the couple fled to Mobile before finally relocating to Paris, where Delphine lived until her death in 1862 at the age of sixty-eight. The remnants of her mansion were purchased in 1838 by Charles Coffin, who hired Pierre Trasfour to rebuild the Lalaurie House in the Empire style.

Over the next few decades, the factual accounts of the "house of horrors" that originally appeared in the *New Orleans Bee* were warped by hearsay and deliberate distortion of the truth. In his book *Ghost Stories of New Orleans* (1946), Jeanne de Lavigne wrote that police and firefighters found enslaved people chained to the walls with their eyes gouged out. He wrote that they also found enslaved people with chunks of flesh sliced from their buttocks. A number of enslaved people were said to have had their fingernails ripped out and their lips sewn shut. It's said one man's intestines had been ripped out and tied around his waist. The most horrific discovery was that of a woman who had a stick protruding from a hole in her skull. Apparently, the stick was used to stir the victim's brains inside her skull. Because the author provided no source for these grisly details, they appear to be part of a folk history of the Lalaurie family that had been generated by local residents years before. Recently, embellishments made by some of the ghost tours have made it even more difficult to separate fact from fiction.

According to local lore, Delphine's sadistic treatment of her enslaved people has left an indelible imprint on her former home. After standing abandoned for a few years, the house became an integrated high school. Later, it became a primary girls' school for an entire year. In 1882, a school for dance and music moved into the building. During this time, female students complained about being attacked by "that woman," who left bruises and scratches on their arms. By the mid-1890s, the Lalaurie House had been turned into an apartment building. In 1894, a tenant who had been complaining about being bothered by "sprites" was found brutally murdered in the house. The man was also convinced that there was a demon in the house who could not rest until he was dead. A motive for his murder was never discovered.

In the late 1890s, most of the tenants were Italian immigrants, several of whom reported being tormented by spirits. One resident claimed they were awakened in the middle of the night by a Black man wearing chains. Several small children told their parents that a "mean lady" chased them with a whip. One young mother was once shocked to see a well-dressed woman standing over her sleeping child.

In the early 1900s, the house was turned into a furniture store. The store had not been open for very long before the owner opened up one morning and found the floor and furniture covered in blood, feces and urine. At first, he suspected that vandals had broken in and done the damage, so he took extra measures to lock up at night. When he found the same filth all over the store a few days later, the owner shut down the store.

Over the next half-century, the house served as a refuge for poverty-stricken men and as the Grand Conservatory of Louisiana. The old house underwent two extensive restorations in the late 1970s. In 2007, actor Nicholas Cage bought the mansion for $3,345,000 but was forced to sell it for $2.5 million in 2009. The Lalaurie House's notoriety made it the ideal setting for several episodes of the third season of the television series *American Horror Story*. Actress Kathy Bates played the role of Delphine Lalaurie.

GENERAL BENJAMIN BUTLER

THE "BEAST"

Benjamin Butler was born in New Hampshire on November, 1818, but he was raised in Lowell, Massachusetts. After graduating from Colby College in Maine in 1828, he was admitted to the Massachusetts Bar in 1840. Butler then set up a very lucrative criminal practice. By the early 1850s, he had ventured into the realm of politics. In 1853, he became a member of the Massachusetts House of Representatives. Six years later, he was elected to the senate of the commonwealth. His military background began in 1839, when he enlisted in the Massachusetts Militia. In 1855, he was promoted to the rank of brigadier general, despite the fact that he had had no formal military training. On May 16, 1861, President Abraham Lincoln appointed him a major general, mostly because he and the Eighth Massachusetts had protected Washington, D.C., in case Maryland seceded from the Union. On June 10, 1861, General Butler's army was defeated in the Battle of Big Bethel in Virginia, one of the first battles of the Civil War.

One of his first acts as commander of Fort Monroe was to apply the label "contraband" to fugitive slaves who sought refuge behind Union lines. In August 1861, General Butler attacked Confederate forces on the Hatteras Inlet in North Carolina and took possession of New Orleans, which had already surrendered to Admiral Farragut on April 25, 1862, without a shot being fired.

General Butler's behavior as the occupational general of New Orleans was criticized by both sides. To let the people of New Orleans know that he would not tolerate any form of resistance, he hanged a man who defaced the American flag and closed down a secessionist newspaper. Under the Federal Confiscation Act, General Butler had the authority to confiscate the property of anyone who would not take an oath of loyalty to the United States. Not only was General Butler ruthless, but he was heartless as well. General Butler closed all of the gambling houses in the city except for those that had purchased a license and had accepted Butler's brother, A.J. Butler, as a "silent partner." This arrangement with his brother netted General Butler large sums of money every week.

BENJAMIN F. BUTLER.

As the occupational general of New Orleans during the Civil War, General Benjamin Butler earned the nickname the "Beast." *Wikimedia Commons*.

Because of these pay-offs, Butler ended up becoming wealthier after he left New Orleans than he was before he got there. He was even said to steal from the homes that he was supposed to be watching.

Butler's most controversial edict was Order 28, which he instituted after a woman stuck her head out of her window and dumped the contents of a chamber pot on the head of Admiral Farragut. Under the new law, any woman who insulted the United States Army would be treated like a prostitute. It turned out that this edict was never enforced. Nevertheless, the women of New Orleans continued showing their distaste for Butler, even going so far as to hire artists to paint the face of General Butler on the bottoms of their chamber pots. It is a small wonder that people called him the "Beast" behind his back.

For a while, Butler's superiors were pleased that he had brought order to New Orleans during the Union Army's occupation of the city, but they eventually decided that the cost was too high. In 1862, he was removed from his post in New Orleans and transferred to the Army of the James in Virginia in November 1863. However, Confederate General G.T. Beauregard bottled up General Butler's army, preventing the general from gaining any momentum during the Bermuda campaign. When General Butler's army was thwarted at Fort Fisher in North Carolina, General Ulysses S. Grant sent him behind the lines to await further orders.

Frustrated because his military career was going nowhere, General Butler resigned his commission on November 30, 1865.

Initially, Butler had more success on the home front. In 1882, he was elected governor of Massachusetts. However, this proved to be his last political victory. Butler's bid for the presidency in 1884 was unsuccessful. He died on January 11, 1893, in Washington, D.C. General Butler had been accused of corruption throughout his life, but none of these charges were ever substantiated in a court of law.

"BRICKTOP"

THE TERROR OF GALLATIN STREET

When one thinks of saloons, sex workers, jazz music and split-second outbursts of violence in the French Quarter, Storyville usually comes to mind. However, the city's original vice district—and the most depraved—was Gallatin Street. This booming economic area in the mid-nineteenth century owed its very existence to the port through which approximately 500,000 immigrants passed between 1841 and 1860. From dusk to dawn, Gallatin Street's rambling dance houses, bordellos and saloons provided a good time to anyone with the time and money. The sailors, soldiers and locals who constituted most of the customers of these dens of iniquity often became the victims of the pickpockets, thieves, harlots and murderers who prowled Gallatin Street, looking for easy prey.

Sex workers—known in the mid-nineteenth century to be working in the city's second most popular industry—thrived on the transient visitors who strolled up and down Gallatin Street. A large number of the sex workers on Gallatin Street were Irish immigrants. The life expectancy of most of these sex workers was four years after they began walking the streets. Because over half of the sex workers had a venereal disease, a cottage industry of "cures" for what was commonly referred to as "the old complaint" soon sprung up. However, contracting a venereal disease was not the only hazard faced by these "public women." Untold numbers of them were murdered for stealing from their "customers" or for refusing to grant their customers sexual favors.

A small number of sex workers on Gallatin Street became murderous themselves. One of the most infamous of these women was a large,

This photograph, taken in 1910, depicts the French Market on Gallatin Street, which was a den of iniquity at the time. *Wikimedia Commons.*

redheaded strumpet named Mary Jane "Bricktop Annie" Jackson, who "worked" on Gallatin Street for almost two years. One could have predicted that Bricktop, born in New Orleans in 1836, would eventually be forced by her circumstances to sell her body in order to survive. Indeed, Bricktop became a "fallen woman" when she was still a thirteen-year-old child and the mistress of a Poydras Street bartender. One day, after living with her for three years, he told her that she was "too hot-headed" and finally drove her out of the house. She inadvertently proved his assessment of her correct by marching into the tavern where he tended the bar and beating him up. She then took up residence in a bordello on Dauphine Street but was forced to leave because of her fiery temper, even though her striking good looks made her one of the establishment's most popular girls.

Bricktop soon found employment in a dance house owned by Archie Murphy. Dance houses in New Orleans were buildings with several stories and a large number of rooms where customers could dance with an attractive young lady for free but were forced to pay high prices for drinks. When these men became too drunk to dance, they were usually robbed and thrown out on the street. While working in Murphy's dance house, Bricktop killed two men, one with a club and another with a wicked-looking knife that had a five-inch blade at each end and a silver handgrip in the middle. Fearing for his own life and those of his customers, Murphy kicked her out after a few weeks.

Bricktop tried to find work at the other dance houses on Gallatin Street, but she did not last very long at any of them. Eventually, she joined up with three other women, America Williams, Ellen Collins and Bridget Fury, who made a living through all sorts of sex work, robbery and picking people's pockets. On November 7, 1859, the women got into big trouble. They were drinking beer at a local beer garden owned by Joe Seidensahl when Bricktop got into an altercation with one of the other patrons, Laurent Fleury. When Fleury slapped Bricktop's face, the other three women jumped him—with knives drawn! Seidensahl tried to stop the brawl, but he was stabbed in the back. Fleury later died from six knife wounds. Ellen Collins escaped before the police arrived, but Bricktop and Williams were taken into custody. Because the authorities could not precisely determine the cause of Fleury's death, the women were set free.

Ironically, true love came to Bricktop while she was in jail awaiting trial for Fleury's murder. Her jailer, John Miller, was a former boxer who had lost an arm in a fight. To make himself look less like an amputee, Miller attached a ball and chain to the stump of his arm. The two were eventually married, but predictably, the couple's marriage was not a good one. Bricktop and Miller's marriage consisted mostly of verbal and physical arguing. On December 5, 1861, Miller, who had been drinking heavily, came home with a cowhide whip. As soon as he walked through the door, he told his wife that she needed a good whipping. His drunken show of force did not have the desired effect. Bricktop grabbed the whip out of his hand and began thrashing him with it. Miller attempted to swing his ball and chain in her direction, but Bricktop grabbed it and pulled him to the floor. Miller made a feeble attempt to reach up and stab Bricktop, but she drew her own special knife and stabbed him multiple times, killing him. Afterward, Bricktop was tried and sentenced to life in prison, but she was released after serving only one year when the military governor of Louisiana, General George F. Shepley, issued blanket pardons to all prisoners. Bricktop, the terror of Gallatin Street, was never seen again.

EUGENE BUNCH

THE GENTLEMAN TRAIN ROBBER

The American train robber has always been enveloped in legend. The source of the public's fascination with these men could lie in the confrontational relationship between man and machine that is celebrated in railroad folk songs like "John Henry." The stereotype of the American train robber is a daring desperado on horseback who, with his gang members, stops one of the mechanized behemoths that roared through the countryside, robs the passengers and the mail car and disappears into the woods or night air. Quite possibly the most romantic of America's train robbers was Eugene Bunch, the "Gentleman Train Robber."

Eugene F. Bunch was born in Mississippi on February 3, 1843. When Bunch was a boy, his parents, who were respected by many people in town, moved to Tangipaphoa Parish, where Bunch received a good education. During the Civil War, Bunch fought with the Third Louisiana Cavalry in the several battles around Port Hudson. At the time, many of his friends believed that he had acquired his fondness for gambling during the war. At the war's end, Bunch opened a school at Amite. In 1869, married a local girl, Flavia Flynn. By 1874, Bunch had tired of teaching, so he and his pregnant wife moved to Gainesville, Texas. He taught in Gainesville for two months before he decided to run for political office. He ran for county clerk and, to his surprise, was elected. He went on to serve in that office for two more years. Then, in his third term, he angered the people of Gainesville by using some of his insider knowledge to make profitable investments in land speculation. By this time, he had also gained a reputation as being something of a ladies' man. When the rumors of his extramarital exploits began circulating through town, Bunch decided not to run for a fourth time for county clerk in 1882.

For the next few years, much of his time was taken up with his old vice—gambling. His family's financial woes exacerbated his marital problems, so he decided to seek out more employment opportunities in Wichita. After two years, he decided to relocate to Fort Worth, where he spent most of his time and money gambling and cavorting with "loose women." While he was there, he also became friends with men who made their living by breaking the law.

When Bunch was forty-three years old, he experienced what many today would refer to as a "midlife crisis." In 1886, Bunch cut off all ties with his family and embarked on a career as a train robber. Between 1886 and 1887, Bunch and a loose assortment of accomplices began robbing trains in North Texas. U.S. Marshall William L. Cabell suspected that the former county clerk was the culprit, but he had no evidence connecting Bunch to the crimes. In November 1888, Bunch pulled off his most audacious train robbery, single-handedly stealing $30,000 in cash and bonds from the United States Express Company in fifteen minutes. The train robbery took place just north of New Orleans in Mississippi. One of Bunch's lovers in Fort Worth identified him as the robber, but the authorities were unable to track him down.

Between 1888 and 1892, Bunch and his cohorts robbed six trains in Mississippi, Louisiana and Texas. Although the authorities could not attach a name to the leader of the gang, Bunch soon became known for his modus operandi. Unlike most of the boorish train robbers in the 1880s, Bunch conducted himself as gentleman. The blue-eyed, soft-spoken outlaw with a black mustache is said to have taken the billfolds of his male victims, but he merely tipped his hat and passed by the women without stealing their handbags. He always introduced himself to them as "Captain J.F. Gerard." The express car messengers reported that the gang leader informed them, in a soft voice, that he would "blow out their brains" if they did not open the safe. After each robbery, Bunch returned to his hideout in the Pearl River area along the state line between Mississippi and Louisiana.

By 1890, Bunch had become the subject of a multistate manhunt. Newspapers speculated, incorrectly, that the bold train robber had hopped a freight train for Tombstone and reappeared in Gainesville as an elderly hobo. Because the heat was on, Bunch decided to "lay low for a while." Then, in 1892, Bunch and two of his gang members—a mentally challenged twenty-one-year-old drifter named Henry Carneguay and a farmer named

Curnell Hobgood—decided to rob another train. In the winter of 1892, the gang made one of their biggest hauls, stealing $20,000 from a southbound train on the New Orleans Northeaster Railroad. Bunch lined up the crew and passengers and was in the process of robbing them when he accidentally dropped a slip of paper that mentioned Bunch's name and the time of arrival of the train at McNeil. One of the passengers noticed the piece of paper on the ground and pressed it into the mud with his shoe. Now the detectives could attach a name to the mysterious bandit who had eluded them for so many years. In April 1892, Bunch and his gang jumped aboard the Illinois Central as it was heading north from New Orleans. Instead of robbing the passengers and the mail car, the bandits opened the express car safe, making off with only cheap jewelry and $500.

Using information garnered from one of Bunch's captured gang members, Henry Carneguay, Detectives Thomas Jackson and C.O. Summers tracked Bunch and Colonel Hopgood down to a spot near Franklinton, a small town in Washington Parish, on August 21, 1892. They were accompanied by three other men. At 9:00 a.m., they arrived at a farm in Muster Grove about eighteen miles east of Franklinton, Louisiana. The men surrounded the farmhouse, but when they found it was empty, they walked around until they spotted Bunch in a clearing. The following account of the shootout appeared in the August 26, 1892 edition of the *Lake Charles Echo*: "Bunch fired his .45 caliber Winchester and started to run. He was then fired upon and filled with buckshot. Hopgood, seeing Bunch fall, threw up his hands and was taken into custody." Bunch was forty-nine years old.

In April 1892, Eugene Bunch stole $500 and some cheap jewelry from an express car that belonged to the Illinois Central Railroad. *Wikimedia Commons.*

News of Bunch's demise at the hands of the detectives and their posse was met with disbelief by many of the citizens of Washington Parish, who said that Colonel Hopgood had shot Bunch while he was asleep in order to collect the $3,000 award on his head. Many also said that the posse had fired their guns at Bunch's corpse to make it look like he had been killed in a gunfight. The public outrage generated by the rumors led to Hopgood's trial for the murder of the man whom many called the "Prince of Outlaws." Not only was Hopgood found not guilty by the jury, but he also did not serve any jail time for his crimes.

Eugene F. Bunch was buried in Morris Cemetery in Franklinton, Louisiana.

DR. ETIENNE DESCHAMPS

THE DEADLY DENTIST OF NEW ORLEANS

In 1887, a suave, fifty-six-year-old dentist named Dr. Etienne Deschamps moved into a two-story brick house at 64 St. Peters Street. Within a few days, he had set up his practice in a single room in his house. The French immigrant's inability to speak English was not a liability because most of his patients spoke French as well. His dental practice thrived, probably because of his reliance on chloroform and an early form of hypnotism called magnetism. He told his patients that the disruption of the flow of magnetic forces in the human body was responsible for a number of afflictions, including diseases. Using a combination of hypnotism and chloroform, Deschamps found that he could ease the pain of his patients in ways that eluded most of the other dentists in New Orleans. Before long, he had expanded his practice outside of New Orleans to include Terrebonne Parish and St. Mary Parish.

On one of his trips through the bayous, Deschamps visited Barataria, Lafitte's hideout. After finding a few coins on the beach, he became obsessed with finding Lafitte's buried plunder. Unlike many of the treasure hunters at that time, who used divining rods to locate buried "treasures," like underground sources of water, Deschamps believed that all he needed was a special person who could reveal the burial site of pirate booty through hypnotism. He was unable to find the ideal conduit until the summer of 1887, when he met Juliette Dietsch, an eleven-year-old girl who lived at 605 Chartres Street in a building now known as the Napoleon House with her father, Jules; her younger sister, Laurence; and her father's eighty-two-year-old mother. Deschamps met the girl's father,

A dentist named Dr. Etienne Deschamps moved into a house on St. Peter Street in 1887. *Wikimedia Commons*.

an unemployed cabinetmaker and carpenter, at a restaurant and quickly formed a close friendship with him, aided in part by the fact that the men had recently emigrated from France and that they lived only a few blocks from each other. When Deschamps learned that his friend was almost out of money, he paid all of Dietsch's bills. Before long, Deschamps began spending a great deal of time at Dietsch's house, where the dentist soon became very close to Dietsch's daughters, especially Juliette. Deschamps also began visiting the girls at Miss Adelaide M. Roux's private school and going on walks with them around New Orleans. When Dietsch observed Deschamps kissing the girls goodnight, he put an end to it.

Nevertheless, the girls continued to visit Deschamps's home. Deschamps ignored his neighbors' warnings that people in the neighborhood were beginning to suspect him of taking advantage of the girls in his house. When Dietsch's mother became ill and he found himself devoting much of his time to her care, Juliette began visiting Deschamps's house alone. On January 29, 1889, Dietsch asked Juliette and Laurence to come to his room. He then instructed them to remove their clothes and lie down in his bed after he gave them chloroform. The next day, the girls were so sick, possibly from chloroform poisoning, that they were unable to go to school.

Top: Juliette Deschamps and her family lived at the Napoleon House in the late 1880s. *Wikimedia Commons.*

Bottom: This is one of the rooms inside the Napoleon House. *Wikimedia Commons.*

On January 30, 1889, between 1:00 and 1:30 p.m., Deschamps arrived at the Dietsch house and shared a late breakfast with Dietsch and his daughters. When they finished eating, Deschamps asked Dietsch if he could take the girls for a walk around New Orleans. Dietsch consented, unaware that his "friend" was going to take his daughters to his upstairs bedroom in his house on St. Peter Street. Once again, Deschamps told the girls to take off their clothes and lie down in bed. He removed the lid from a bottle of chloroform and asked Juliette to inhale. Fighting the urge to turn her head away from the foul-smelling bottle, Juliette took a deep breath and closed her eyes. After a minute or so, she told Laurence and Deschamps that she had a vision of God, the Virgin Mary and Jackson Square. Deschamps then told Juliette to breathe in the chloroform through her mouth and her nose. After a few minutes, Juliette was still conscious, so Deschamps poured the remaining contents of the bottle onto his handkerchief and placed it over the girl's nose. She soon fell into a deep slumber.

After Juliette fell asleep, Deschamps left his house to replenish his supply of chloroform, which could be purchased in small quantities from local apothecaries. Laurence, who had refused to take the chloroform Deschamps had offered her, watched the man put two empty chloroform bottles in his jacket pocket and leave the house. Deschamps walked over to Majeau's drugstore on Bourbon Street, only three blocks away, and bought more chloroform. As soon as Deschamps returned to his bedroom, he removed his clothes and walked over to Juliette's motionless body on the bed. He poured some of the chloroform on a handkerchief and placed it over her mouth. He then gave Laurence a bundle of dental tools and told her to deliver them to her father. When she left the house, Deschamps shut the door and locked it. After returning home, Laurence told her father that Juliette was asleep and that Deschamps was going to die. Dietsch immediately rushed out of the house and headed over to Deschamps's house on St. Peter Street. He banged on the door, but no one answered, so he went back home and told Laurence to accompany him to the dentist's house. Once they arrived, Dietsch and Laurence knocked loudly on the door so they could wake up Deschamps if he was asleep. The commotion woke up Deschamps's next-door neighbor Charles Serra. After Dietsch explained that his daughter Juliette was in the dentist's house, the men walked over to Deschamps's house; while Dietsch banged on the door, Serra looked through the window but could not see anyone inside. Convinced that his daughter was in the house, Dietsch hurried over to the police station and told the officer at the front desk that his daughter was locked inside Deschamps's house. Two officers were dispatched to the house on St. Peter Street. Once they broke through the door, the men made their way to the bedroom, where they found Deschamps and Juliette lying on the bed. The officers immediately detected the strong odor of the chloroform fumes in the room. Deschamps had apparently tried to stab himself with a four-inch dental tool. Dietsch entered the room a few seconds later and was shocked to find his nude daughter lying on the bed. Inside the room, the police found four letters to Deschamps signed by Juliette Dietsch. Deschamps was placed on a stretcher and taken to Charity Hospital. At 6:30 p.m., Dr. Yves LeMonnier received a phone call informing him that a rape had occurred at Deschamps's house on St. Peter Street and that he should go there as soon as possible.

Dr. Etienne Deschamps purchased a bottle of chloroform, similar to this one, in a New Orleans pharmacy. *Wikimedia Commons*.

At 6:15 p.m., Dr. LeMonnier arrived at the Charity Hospital, where he gave Deschamps a thorough examination. The doctor observed that Deschamps had punctured his own lung with the four-inch dental tool—a "toothpicker"—and had also stabbed himself twice in the chest. Deschamps was released the next morning and transported to Judge Guy Dreux's courtroom on the first floor of the Cabildo. Deschamps informed the judge that he had attempted to transform Juliette into a "beautiful subject" by magnetizing her. He failed, he said, because she was not a virgin. Deschamps also admitted to the judge that when he told Juliette that he was going to die by suicide, she replied that she was going to kill herself, too.

Deschamps said that Juliette then picked up a bottle of chloroform from the table and poured the contents on a handkerchief. Lying down on the bed, Juliette held the handkerchief under her nose and took several deep breaths. After she fell asleep, Deschamps said that he drank some of the chloroform and fell asleep within a few minutes. Deschamps ended his testimony by stating that when he found that Juliette was dead, he tried to take his own life by stabbing himself several times. He believed that Juliette had killed herself because he had told her he was going to kill himself. At the end of his testimony, Deschamps entered a plea of not guilty.

Dr. LeMonnier conducted the autopsy on Juliette's body before her funeral. He determined that the child had died from inhaling chloroform. The doctor also confirmed Deschamps's belief that Juliette was not a virgin. Because Jules Dietsch was unable to pay for his daughter's funeral, money was raised by a jeweler named J. Julius Weinfurter. Juliette's body was taken to John Bonnot's funeral home on January 31, 1890. Hundreds of mourners gathered outside to pay their respects. At the end of the viewing, Juliette's body was taken to St. Louis Cemetery No. 1 for burial in an unmarked tomb. On the same day as Juliette's funeral, Deschamps was transported to Orleans Parish Prison, where he was treated for his self-inflicted wounds and chloroform poising in the infirmary.

Above: Dr. Etienne Deschamps was transported to Judge Guy Dreux's courtroom on the first floor of the Cabildo in 1889. *Wikimedia Commons*.

Left: This is the interior of the Cabildo. *Wikimedia Commons*.

Deschamps's trial was held at the courthouse on Camp Street. While awaiting trial, Deschamps tried to kill himself multiple times by diving headfirst off the water closet, by hanging himself in his cell and by jumping over the railing on the second floor of the prison. Deschamps's trial began on April 29, 1889. James Dowling, his court-appointed lawyer, had informed Judge Marr that it would take him a month to prepare for the trial. Midway through the trial, Deschamps replaced Dowling with Judge Alfred Roman, who spoke French. On March 29, 1890, the jury found Deschamps guilty of murder. Judge Roman appealed the verdict on

April 7, 1890. On February 21, 1891, the board of pardons appointed a commission of physicians to determine whether Deschamps was insane.

On March 11, 1897, the board of pardons ruled that Deschamps was not insane at the time of Juliette's murder. Lieutenant Governor James Jeffries upheld the board's verdict and signed Deschamps's death warrant on March 24, 1892. Deschamps's execution was set for May 13, 1892. On the day of Deschamps's execution, Deputy Sheriff Edgar White walked into Deschamps's cell and woke him up at 5:00 a.m. At 7:00 a.m., a Jesuit priest entered Deschamps's cell to take his confession. Deschamps said that he would pray only to God. Around 8:00 a.m., Deschamps ate a plate of eggs for breakfast. At 9:00 a.m., Deschamps got dressed in his hanging clothes—a white shirt, striped pants and slippers. He then walked to the third-floor chapel and received the sacrament of Communion. At 1:05 p.m., Deschamps was escorted down to the gallery, where the witnesses of the execution were standing. Suddenly, Deschamps turned to Dr. LeMonnier, who had stalwartly insisted that Deschamps was not insane, and called him a murderer. The condemned man also declared, "I am innocent!" He was then taken to the gangway, where the executioner, known only as "Hangman Taylor," was waiting for him. At 1:10 p.m., after the hangman placed the noose around Deschamps's neck, Sheriff Villere asked him if he had any last words. All Deschamps said was "Adieu." At 1:10 p.m., Deschamps was hanged. At 4:00 pm., Deschamps's corpse was taken to Holt Cemetery, a potter's field, and was buried.

THE ROBERT CHARLES RIOTS

Pinning blame for a particular crime on a specific person is usually a matter of tracking down the culprit by means of good police work. However, in the case of mob violence, where crimes such as theft or murder are committed by masses of people, narrowing down the instigator to a single person can be difficult at best. According to the article "Mob Violence: Cultural-Societal Sources, Instigators, Group Processes, and Participants," by Leonard D. Eron, Jacquelyn H. Gentry, et al., people engage in mob violence because of "frustration, hostility, exploding anger, and the desire to hurt." At different times in American history, specific racial groups have become the targets of mob violence. Such a riot occurred in New Orleans in 1900.

Robert Charles was born a freeman in 1865 to parents who were enslaved at the time. When Robert was born, his parents were sharecroppers who were different from most Black Americans at that time, because both of them could read and write and because his father was a registered voter. When Charles moved to New Orleans from Mississippi, he was a self-educated man. People who know him when he was young said that he loved to read. Before long, he became a political activist, encouraging Black people to move to Liberia. On July 3, 1900, he was sitting on a porch with his nineteen-year-old roommate, Leonard Pierce, in a predominantly white neighborhood. The two young men were drinking while they were waiting for a few of their friends to get off work. After a short while, three white policemen, Sergeant Jules C. Aucoin, Officer August T. Mora and Officer Joseph D. Cantrelle, walked up to the two men and asked them what they were doing there and how long they had been waiting on the porch. One of the young men replied that they were waiting for a friend. Then Charles stood up, which one of the police officers took as a hostile move. Officer Mora grabbed Charles and struggled with him for a few minutes. What started out as a scuffle escalated into a full-fledged gunfight when Mora attempted to stop Charles by beating him on the head and body with his billy club. Charles and Mora pulled out their guns and began shooting. Both men were shot in their legs. One of the three policemen held Pierce at bay while Charles ran toward his apartment at 1208 Saratoga Street. Following the blood trail Charles left behind, the policemen cornered him at his home the next morning. On July 24, 1900, at 3:00 a.m., as soon as Charles spotted the officers standing in front of his house, he began shooting at them with his .38-caliber Winchester rifle. He hit Day in the heart and another police officer, Peter Lamb, in the head. As the other officers took cover, Charles made his escape.

The next day, while the police were conducting a manhunt for Robert Charles, a crowd of white people converged on the site on Fourth Street where Charles had shot and killed the two policemen. Before long, they began rallying for the capture and lynching of Robert Charles. On July 25, the acting mayor, William L. Mehle, made matters worse by offering a $250 reward for Charles's capture. Local newspapers escalated the situation even more when they blamed Black people for the unrest. On the night of July 25, armed white mobs began roaming the streets, killing three Black people and severely wounding six others. Approximately fifty people were slightly injured. The racial turmoil came to a bloody end on Friday, July 27, when the police, aided by white vigilantes, trapped Charles in a house at 1208 Saratoga Street. For a short period that seemed to last for hours, Charles and the police exchanged gunfire. At 5:00 p.m., when it seemed that Charles could go on shooting at them forever, a fire captain and several other men sneaked into the basement and set fire to an old mattress. Overcome by the smoke seeping into the first floor from the basement, Charles fled the house. A Tulane University medical student was one of the volunteers who shot and killed Charles. Even though Charles was obviously dead, a group of angry bystanders began beating his body and riddling it with gunfire.

Before he took his last breath, Robert Charles had shot 27 white people, killing 7; 4 of the casualties were policemen. The militia was not the only group of white people who pursued Robert Charles. Hundreds of the white residents of New Orleans took to the streets, barging into the homes of Black citizens; setting fire to public buildings, including two schoolhouses;

The house where Robert Charles was killed stood on Saratoga Street. *Wikimedia Commons*.

and attacking Black people with clubs. By the time they were finished, at least 20 innocent people were dead, and 50 were wounded. To prevent further bloodshed, New Orleans mayor Paul Capdeville deputized 1,500 special police. He also requested aid from the state militia.

The Robert Charles Riots did not go unnoticed by the national press. The consequences of the blanket coverage of the riots were both positive and negative. In northern cities like Boston, Massachusetts, funds were raised for the injured Black victims of the riots. However, racial hatred across the United States escalated as well. A white supremacist group called the Turtles was formed in New Orleans soon after the riots. In addition, Louisiana passed an anti-miscegenation law in 1908. In downtown New Orleans, a segregated parish was created.

For years, the Robert Charles Riots were blamed entirely on the young Black man who had confronted the police who were harassing him. However, blame must also be placed on the white people who used the riots as an excuse to vent their racial hatred on the Black residents of New Orleans. Once the facts of the riots are known, it becomes clear that there is plenty of blame to go around.

"LEATHER BRITCHES" SMITH AND THE 1912 GRABOW LABOR RIOT

In the early 1900s, the piney woods of western Louisiana and East Texas were a major source of economic growth for the people living in that part of the South and contributed to the creation of the "New South." Large stands of shortleaf, longleaf and loblolly pine trees attracted lumbermen from all over the country. Although the people who labored in the woods and in the lumber mills certainly benefited from the arrival of the lumber companies, they experienced hardship as well. During periods of overproduction and price fluctuations, employers cut labor costs by reducing hours of operation. Poor working conditions also generated unrest among workers that led to the creation of unions and eventually culminated in the Louisiana-Texas Lumber War of 1911–12.

The strife between lumber workers and lumber mill owners began in August 1912, when thirty lumber mills in East Texas went on strike. For the most part, the owners of the lumber companies dealt with the situation by firing and blacklisting union members, replacing the striking workers with immigrant strikebreakers and resorting to violence, including the hiring of private armies to put down strikes.

The most famous confrontation between lumber companies and workers took place in Grabow, Louisiana. On July 7, 1912, the president of the Timber Workers, Arthur L. Emerson, and seventy-five workers tried to enlist more union members at the Canon sawmill, but nonunion workers interrupted his speech by beating on buckets. Undaunted by their unfriendly reception at the Canon sawmill, Emerson and his group traveled to the

In the early 1900s, immense stands of longleaf pine trees attracted hundreds of lumbermen from all over the country to eastern Texas and western Louisiana. *Wikimedia Commons.*

Galloway Lumber Company's mill at Grabow, which had been on strike for about a month. Once again, Emerson tried to speak to the workers, but he was drowned out by nonunion workers pounding on buckets. Suddenly, a shot was fired. For the next ten minutes, both sides shot at each other. By the time the gunfire ended, thirty men had been either killed or wounded. Two of the strikers who died in the melee were Zach Martin and Decatur Hall. Other casualties included A.T. Vincent and an unknown immigrant. Two of the wounded men, Bud Hickman and Ed Brown, received bullet wounds to the chest.

After the Grabow Riot, Sheriff Henry Reid and Deputies Del Charian, Paul McMillan, Ike Meadows and James Broxton arrested nearly one hundred workers, even though most of the evidence pointed to mill owner John Galloway and his henchmen. Of those arrested, only sixty men and three women—all of whom were union workers—were indicted. For several months, all sixty men were crammed into a single cell in the hottest part of the summer with only a single faucet and toilet. They were never allowed outside of the jail cell. Most of their food was provided by women from the surrounding communities. Nine of the accused men were tried between October 7 and October 31, 1912. At the end of the trial, all of the defendants were acquitted. All of the charges against the remaining defendants were dropped as well.

One of the rioters who was not arrested was an eccentric rogue named Charles "Leather Britches" Smith. His name came from his habit of wearing filthy buckskin pants almost every day. He was frequently sighted around Merryville, Louisiana, wearing two pistols strapped to his waist. People feared Smith because he was reputed to have killed several men in West Texas but had somehow eluded capture.

"Leather Britches" Smith participated in the Grabow Riot in 1912. *Gracen Deerman.*

Because Smith had once worked as a logger for $1.50 a day, he allied himself with the striking lumber workers. On July 7, 1912, Smith stood by Emerson's side. During the heat of the riot, Emerson knelt down and fired his rifle at the sawmill. As the smoke cleared a few minutes later, Smith ran off into the woods. The deputies doggedly pursued Smith but were unable to find him until they heard a rumor that he had taken refuge in an abandoned sawmill. On September 25, 1912, they found him asleep underneath a log car. In a loud, commanding voice, one of the deputies ordered Smith to surrender. Instead, Smith grabbed for his pistol but was gunned down in a hail of bullets. Smith was shot four times in the back and once in the neck. Not everyone accepted the official version of Smith's demise, however. Rumors soon began circulating around Merryville that Smith had been shot by his partner, Curnell Hobgood, while he was asleep. To cover up the murder, the deputies riddled his body with bullets.

Smith's unconventional burial was very much in line with his unconventional life. The citizens of Merryville were divided over whether he should be buried in the Merryville Cemetery. They finally arrived at a compromise and buried him along the fence line with a cedar board marking his grave. In 2010, someone erected a gravestone that resembled the cedar marker. This stone, in turn, was eventually replaced with a more conventional headstone.

THE "VOODOO MURDERS"
OF CLEMENTINE BARNABET

Axe murderers are regarded by many people to be the most brutal type of murderers. One reason is the implication that, in the eyes of these killers, their victims are nothing more than logs or trees. Of course, the most obvious reason for the revulsion associated with axe murderers is the blood that coats their crime scenes. Writing in *Country Roads Magazine* in 2022, author Chris Turner Neal said that a string of axe murders occurred across the United States in towns like Colorado Springs and Villisca, Iowa, between 1910 and 1912. One of the most horrific of these murders took place in towns located near the Southern Pacific Railroad line in Texas and Louisiana. In 1911, an abusive husband and father named Raymond Barnabet was arrested for the murders of Alexander, Mimi, Joachim and Agnes Andrus. They were killed with an axe that police found on the property. The authorities released Barnabet two days later because of the lack of evidence connecting him to the crime. Several months later, evidence turned in by a friend of his lover led to his arrest. This "friend" claimed that Barnabet's lover, a woman named Diana Porter, gave her information about the axe murders that implicated Barnabet. However, because Diana and Barnabet accused the friend of lying, the police decided to interview his teenage children, Clementine and Zepherin, and their mother, Nina, who had recently separated from him. During Barnabet's trial, Clementine and Zepherin claimed that the night of the Andrus family murders, their father had come home from work wearing clothes splattered with blood and brain matter. Diana Porter took the stand

and contradicted everything Barnabet's children had sworn to in court, but the jury found him guilty of murder anyway.

Raymond's jail time was cut short by the axe murder of another Lafayette family. This time, the authorities placed the blame on Raymond's daughter, Clementine, who was working as a maid not far from the murder scene. A search of Clementine's room produced some very incriminating evidence: a bloody dress, apron and underwear. Blood was also found on the door latch. Clementine told the sheriff that her father had wiped his bloody hands on her clothes, but he didn't believe her. Because Clementine's brother had an alibi on the night of the murder, Clementine was taken to jail.

However, in January 1912, while Clementine and her father were sitting in jail, three more families were murdered by an axe-wielding assailant. On January 19, 1912, police arrested Zepherin Barnabet for the axe murder of Marie Warner and her three children in Crowley. That same night, Felix Broussard; his wife, Matilda; and their three children were axed to death. This time, the killer wrote a misquoted verse from Psalm 9 in pencil on the wall and signed it "Human Five." In the newspapers' coverage of this particular murder, they referred to the culprits as the "Human Five Gang" and connected the crime to the practice of Voodoo.

In April, the mounting pressure brought on by the negative publicity in the newspapers became too much for Clementine. On the same day that the grand jury convened, April 5, 1912, she admitted to having killed the

Byers, Randall and Andrus families with an axe. She professed to being the leader of the Church of the Sacrificed and claimed she committed the murders with the help of accomplices, none of whom were ever found. Clementine said that as a voodoo priestess, she presided over voodoo rites and acts of sexual perversion. She credited the voodoo charms she had purchased with giving her the fortitude to kill her victims. Despite the inconsistencies in her account of the way she committed the murders, charges were filed against Clementine on April 14, 1912. Tellingly, while she awaited trial, axe murders were reported in Mississippi and Texas, but no more axe murders were committed in Louisiana at this time. Despite her lawyer's

Self-professed voodoo priestess Clementine Barbare confessed to murdering several people with an axe in 1912. Gracen Deerman.

insistence that none of her confession could be believed, Clementine was found guilty and sentenced to life in prison. Psychologists who examined Clementine after her confession testified that she was sane.

The facts of Clementine's case became even murkier thanks to sensationalistic newspaper articles claiming that she had actually committed more murders than she had admitted to. Suspicions regarding the actual existence of the Church of the Sacrificed arose when investigators discovered that all the other church members she had named had alibis for the nights of the murders. Clementine began serving her life sentence at Angola State Penitentiary in 1912. She made an attempt to escape from prison on July 31, 1913, but was recaptured a few hours later. Despite her failed escape attempt, Clementine was allowed to work outside of Angola Prison as a cane cutter in 1918. She was released from prison for good behavior on August 15, 1923. In their book *The Man from the Train*, authors Bill and Rachel McCarthy James theorized that Clementine did not serve out her full prison term because the authorities were not convinced that she was really guilty. They also suggested that most, if not all, of the crimes attributed to Clementine were really perpetrated by a German immigrant named Paul Mueller, who killed as many as ninety people, including people Clementine was accused of murdering, with the blunt side of an axe while living along the railroad.

THE NEW ORLEANS MAFIA

Most people prefer to think of New Orleans as the "Big Easy," a place where people can visit to cut loose with drinks, fine Cajun cuisine and jazz joints. However, New Orleans is also the first city in the United States where the traditional Sicilian mafia gained a foothold in the late 1890s, even reaching the White House.

By the late 1800s, New Orleans was overrun with criminals, many of whom were of Italian descent. A significant percentage of them were mafiosi—members of the Black Hand—who preyed on the hardworking, productive Italians living in the French Quarter. The first high-profile crime committed by the mafia was the murder of New Orleans police chief David Hennessy, who got caught in the crossfire between two powerful New Orleans families: the Provenzano and Matranga families. The Provenzano family had no connection to organized crime. They made their fortune controlling the docks where goods from Central and South America came through. On the other hand, the Matranga family had very strong ties to the New Orleans mafia, specializing in labor racketeering and extortion. Many of their victims were dockworkers, including members of the Provenzano family, who occasionally paid tribute to them. To keep the peace, the Provenzano family gave the Matranga family their cut of the waterfront business and got involved in the grocery and produce business. However, when the Matranga family tried to take over the Provenzanos' grocery and produce business, both families hired mafiosi to fight their "war." On October 17, 1888, Tony Matranga and two of his men were ambushed at Claiborne Avenue and Esplanade Street. Peter and Joe Provenzano, along with three of their men, were arrested.

This incident occurred around the same time that David Hennessy became police chief. He suspected that the Provenzano family were "in the right," so he focused his investigation on the illegal activities of the Matranga family. Not surprisingly, Hennessy began receiving death threats. Instead of being intimidated by the threats against his life, Hennessy publicly announced that he was going to present his evidence at the trial of the Provenzano brothers. On October 14, 1890, just a couple of days before the trial, Hennessy left his office and began walking to his home on Girod Street. Walking alongside of him was Captain William J. O'Connor. When the pair reached Girod Street, O'Connor left Hennessy and began walking to his own home. Suddenly, O'Connor heard the thundering blast from a shotgun and three shots from a revolver. He rushed back to the place where he had left Hennessy on Girod Street, and he found him sitting on a stoop with blood gushing from bullet holes in the left side of his body. When O'Connor asked Hennessy who shot him, he replied, "Dagoes," and passed out. Hennessy was rushed to Charity Hospital, where he died the next morning.

The murder of David Hennessy created a firestorm in New Orleans. The most prominent political leaders in Louisiana attended the funeral, which was held in the council chamber at city hall. Thousands of mourners lined the streets as the funeral procession made its way to the cemetery. As rumors of lynching people connected with the mafia began circulating through the city, a number of Italians published notices in the newspapers denying any personal connection to the Black Hand. Nineteen Italians, many of whom were members of the Matranga family, were charged with Hennessy's murder. Their case went to trial on February 17, 1891; on March 12, the jury foreman announced that they were unable to agree on three of the defendants' charges, but they acquitted the remaining sixteen. Within a few hours, evidence was found that indicated some of the jurors had been paid off by the mafia.

Outrage at the jury's verdict was almost palpable. Hundreds of Italian citizens gathered outside of the statue of Henry Clay at the junction of Royal and St. Charles Streets. After receiving their orders from three of the organizers, hundreds of people, armed with rifles and shotguns, marched to the prison. Captain Davis locked all of the prisoners in their cells except for the Italians, who were told to find a good hiding place. The mob found the gates to the prison locked, but they were able to get in by smashing down a wooden door on Maris Street. Several men rushed through the door, waving sheets of paper with the names of eleven suspects written on them. All of the suspects were dragged to the yard of the women's prison, where they were all shot or hanged. The next morning, most of the local newspapers praised the "mob justice" that had taken place in their city. Although the fate of the members of the Matranga family did not remove the presence of the mafia in New Orleans, it did force the leaders to stay out of the limelight.

Another violent episode in the history of mafia activity in New Orleans occurred at the Beauregard-Keyes House at 113 Chartres Street. In 1825, the nuns of the Ursuline Convent sold the plot of land to a developer. In 1826, James Lambert built the house for an auctioneer named Joseph Le Carpenter. The Creole cottage is distinctive for its Greek Revival features, including a Palladia façade. The next owner of the house was John A. Merle, the consul of Switzerland, who moved into the house in 1833 with his wife, Anais Philippon. The house changed owners again in 1865, when a grocer named Dominique Lanata purchased it as a rental property. His first tenant was Confederate general Pierre Gustave Toutant Beauregard, who lived in the house from 1866 to 1868. In 1945, author Frances Parkinson Keyes purchased the house that now bears her name. She wrote thirty novels while living there, including *Dinner at Antoine's* and *The Chess Players*.

Built in 1826, the Beauregard-Keyes House was the site of a mafia shoot-out on June 17, 1908. *Wikimedia Commons*.

Author Francis Parkinson Keyes restored the garden of the Beauregard-Keyes House in the mid-twentieth century. *Wikimedia Commons.*

In 1904, the Lanata family sold the house to the Giaccona family. The house is located in the heart of what became known as "Little Palermo" because of the large number of Italians living there. Many of these people were victimized by members of the mafia, who specialized in extortion. Their modus operandi involved sending a note or letter to someone, often an immigrant, demanding money to prevent themselves or their loved ones from being abducted or murdered. Some people even had their houses or stores dynamited. One of these immigrants who was targeted by the mafia was Pietro Giacona, who purchased the house on Chartres Street in 1904. He earned a living making and selling wine from the basement of the house. On June 17, 1908, two Black Hand thugs, Giovani Barreco and Ciro Cusimano, showed up at Pietro's basement door at 9:00 p.m. with two other men. In the past, Giacona knew, Barreco and Cusimano had frequently requested food and wine but rarely paid for it. On this particular night, Cusimano demanded $50 from Giacona, and Barreco demanded $100. For Pietro, this was the last straw. He was sick and tired of being taken advantage of by these criminals. When they told him they were hungry, Giacona told them to go the gallery so that his adult son, Corrado, could make them some eggs. Pietro then excused himself and went upstairs. While he was gone, the mafiosi tried to force Corrado to give them money. When the young man refused, Cusimano reached into his pocket for a gun. Seeing his chance, Corrado jumped up and ran to the door. Cusimano fired once but missed. As Corrado left, Pietro returned to the gallery with a rifle in his hand. He immediately fired and shot the two men waiting out in the yard, killing one, Nuzio Barreco, and wounding the other. The police arrived ten

FACSIMILE OF A TYPICAL BLACK HAND LETTER, WHICH, TRANS-
LATED, READS:

*This is the second time that I have warned you. Sunday at ten o'clock in the
morning, at the corner of Second Street and Third Avenue, bring three hundred dollars
without fail. Otherwise we will set fire to you and blow you up with a bomb. Consider this matter well, for this is the last warning I will give you.*
                    I sign the Black Hand.

Around the turn of the century, the mafia, also known as the "Black Hand," extorted money from Italian immigrants by passing them notes like this one, which demands the payment of $300. *Wikimedia Commons.*

minutes later. Both Pietro and Corrado were indicted for murder but were later found innocent. Both men were praised by members of the Italian community for standing up to the Black Hand.

Sicilian-born "Silver Dollar Sam" Carollo took over the Black Hand following Charles Matranga's retirement in 1922. He immediately took over Matranga's bootlegging operations and declared war against rival bootlegging gangs. It was not long before Carollo exerted considerable political influence in New Orleans. The story goes that when Al Capone showed up at a New Orleans train station with the intention of demanding that Carollo supply the Chicago mob with imported liquor, Carollo met Capone with several policemen, who broke the fingers of Capone's bodyguards and sent them all back to Chicago.

In 1934, Carollo made agreements with several mafia heads and Senator Huey Long to bring slot machines into Louisiana. Carollo was arrested on a narcotics charge in 1938 and was scheduled to be deported in 1940, but his deportation was delayed because of the United States' entry into World War II. Carollo continued running the New Orleans mafia until he was finally deported in 1947. He returned briefly to the United States in 1949 but departed again in 1950. Carollo lived in Sicily until 1970, when he returned to the United States. Carollo died of a heart attack in 1972.

Carlos "Little Man" Marcello was New Orleans's next mafia boss. Born in Tunisia in 1910, he moved to Jefferson Parish, a suburb of New Orleans, Louisiana, as an infant with his family. His parents changed his name from Calogero Minacore to Carlos Marcello. He began committing petty thefts in the French Quarter as a child and continued stealing well into his teenage years. In 1928, he was arrested for selling twenty-three pounds of marijuana. He was sentenced to ten months in prison but served only two months because of a deal he made with Governor Huey Long. In the late 1940s, he partnered with Frank Costello, the leader of the Genovese crime family in New York City, and took control of all of the slot machines in the region. As don of the New Orleans mob, Marcello made millions of dollars from vice rackets in Louisiana and other states along the Gulf Coast, including Texas. According to the Senate's Kefauver Committee, Marcello paid off sheriffs, marshals and other law enforcement officers for their failure to enforce gambling laws and statutes related to vice.

Marcello soon found out that President John F. Kennedy and his brother Attorney General Robert Kennedy were impervious to payoffs. On April 4, 1961, Robert Kennedy deported Marcello to Guatemala, his mother's fictional birthplace. When he returned to New Orleans two months later, his hatred of the Kennedys fueled suspicion that Marcello and his mafia cohorts had orchestrated the assassination of President John F. Kennedy on November 22, 1963. In November 1963, Marcello was tried for conspiracy to defraud the United States by procuring a fake Guatemalan birth certificate and for conspiring to obstruct the United States' attempt to deport him, but he was acquitted a few weeks later on both charges. In October 1964, Marcello was accused of "fixing" a juror, Rudolph Heitler, and seeking the murder of a government witness, but he was acquitted of both of those charges as well. In 1978, the House Select Committee on Assassinations found that Marcello had the motive, means and opportunity to have President Kennedy assassinated, but the committee was unable to produce direct evidence of Marcello's involvement. However, the committee did consider Marcello one of the ten most powerful mafia leaders in the United States.

In 1981, Marcello, Aubrey W. Young, Charles E. Roemer and two other men were indicted in the U.S. District Court of Louisiana in New Orleans on charges of conspiracy, racketeering and mail and wire fraud in their plan to bribe state officials. Marcello died in 1993 at the age of eighty-three after serving his prison term.

Born on November 23, 1923, Anthony Carollo was the son of a mafioso moneylender, Silvestro Carollo. After serving in World War II, Carollo became the owner of an Italian restaurant in New Orleans. In May 1994, Anthony Carollo and sixteen members of the Marcello, Gambino and Genovese families were caught up in an FBI sting called Operation Hard Crust. The men were accused of racketeering, illegal gambling, conspiracy and infiltrating the video poker industry. Anthony Carollo was imprisoned from 1995 to 1998 and died on February 1, 2007. Anthony Carollo's brother Joseph Carollo took over the crime family in 1983 but stepped down in 1990.

THE AXEMAN OF NEW ORLEANS

Hundreds of police departments across the country are haunted by the unsolved crimes in their files. The faces of the victims and their loved ones never completely go away, especially for those officers who have doggedly pursued the culprits for much of their careers. For example, the Jack the Ripper murders have received a great deal of attention over the years. In New Orleans, the eighteen-month murder spree of a serial killer known only as the "Axeman" still sends shivers down the spines of the residents of the Big Easy.

In the nineteenth century, thousands of Sicilians immigrated to Louisiana because of the area's great need for cheap labor, especially on the sugarcane plantations. In the 1880s and 1890s, 80 percent of the immigrants who arrived in New Orleans were Sicilians. Many of the immigrants working on the plantations saved enough money so that within two or three years, they could move to the city and open up a shop, like a flower shop or a grocery store. Around the turn of the twentieth century, many of these "swarthy" Sicilians became of the targets of prejudiced residents of Louisiana. Some of these Sicilians were lynched by angry mobs. By the 1900s, a large number of Sicilians had moved to the lower French Quarter. In fact, for many years, the area from Jackson Square to Esplande Avenue, between Decatur and Chartres Streets, was called "Little Palermo." The business of choice for many of these immigrants was the grocery business. By 1920, Italians owned and operated half of all the grocery stores in New Orleans. For eighteen months between 1918 and 1919, many of these small business owners fell prey to a serial killer known only as the Axeman of New Orleans.

The first murder took place on May 22, 1918. An Italian grocer named Joe Maggio returned home at 2:00 a.m. after a long evening of drinking. His wife, Catherine, had already fallen asleep by the time he climbed into bed. Joseph and his wife lived in the same house as his two brothers, Jacob and Andrew. Two hours after Joseph returned home, Jacob was awakened by a moaning sound coming from Joseph's room next door. Curiosity got the best of Jacob, so he opened the door. The scene inside the room kept Jacob awake for the next several nights. Both Joseph and his wife had their throats cut. Joseph was lying halfway off his bed; Catherine was sprawled on the floor, not far from a bloody razor and axe. The safe was open, but Catherine's jewelry and the $100 under Joseph's pillow were untouched. The murderer had apparently entered the apartment through a hole he had made with a chisel in a panel of the back door.

A few weeks later, on June 27, 1918, the killer struck again. A grocer named Louis Besumer, who lived in the back of his store with his common-law wife, Annie Harriet Lowe, did not answer the door when a baker named John Zanca knocked on the door. He was delivering some bread that Besumer had ordered. Zanca walked around to the back door. All of a sudden, the door burst open, and Besumer staggered through the doorway with blood gushing from a horrible wound to his head. To keep the injured man from falling, Zanca grabbed his shoulders and helped him back to his bedroom, where he found Annie lying on the bed in a pool of blood. She had been struck in the head with an axe. Once the shock of his discoveries subsided, Zanca called the police station and Charity Hospital. Besumer had suffered a concussion, and Annie slipped into a deep coma.

When the police arrived on the scene of the crime, they found the axe, which belonged to Besumer, in the bathroom. Because of a collection of letters written in German that were found in a chest, the police suspected him of having committed espionage. After Annie regained consciousness, she accused Besumer of being a German spy. She died in August 1918 following surgery. Besumer was arrested and served nine months in jail, but he was acquitted on May 1, 1919.

On the night of August 5, 1918, Mrs. Edward Schneider, who was eight months pregnant, had an unexpected visitor. When her husband returned home from work after midnight, he was horrified to find his wife lying in bed, unconscious, with a deep slash in her scalp. She was rushed to Charity Hospital. Despite her injuries, she gave birth two days later. She told the police that she awoke to see a large, dark figure standing over her. Investigators found no evidence in the bedroom, but they were confused by the Axeman's change in his modus operandi: the assailant had entered the room through a window instead of a back door.

Five days later, an older man named Joseph Romano was the Axeman's next victim. He was living in a house with his two nieces, who stayed in the room next door. On the night of August 10, the girls heard a commotion coming from their uncle's room. One of the girls, Pauline, slowly opened the door and looked toward the bed, where she saw a tall, dark man wearing a dark suit and hat standing next to her uncle's bed. Alarmed, Pauline screamed. Her sudden appearance surprised the intruder so much that he dashed out of the room. At the same time, Pauline saw her uncle, with blood streaming down his forehead, stumbling toward her. He was able to make it to the parlor before finally collapsing on the floor. As Pauline and her sister, Mary, helped their uncle into a chair, he told them to call Charity Hospital.

Romano died in the hospital two days later. When the police scoured Romano's property, they discovered a bloody hatchet in the yard. They found the intruder had also removed a panel in the back door. It appeared that someone had gone through Romano's house, looking for something of value, but nothing was missing.

Soon, panic took hold of the city of New Orleans. The police department received a number of phone calls regarding the discovery of axes and chisels outside the doors of residents. In September, Paul Durrell informed the police that someone had tried to break down his back door. After that phone call, the Axeman dropped out of sight for several months. On March 10, 1919, a grocer named Charles Cortimiglia was with his wife, Rosie, and their two-year-old daughter, Mary, in Gretna, Louisiana. Later that night, a neighbor, Lorlando Jordano, heard screams coming from the Cortimiglias' house. After Jordano forced his way into the house, Rosie informed him that she was asleep in bed when she awoke in the early morning hours to find her husband trying to fight off a man with an axe. After subduing Charles Cortimiglia, the assailant attacked Rosie and her daughter with an axe. Both Rosie and her daughter were taken to the hospital, where they were treated for skull fractures. Mary's parents survived their ordeal, but little Mary died.

Once Rosie was fit enough to talk to police, she blamed the crimes on grocer Lorlando Jordano and their eighteen-year-old son, Frank. Even though Charles Cortimiglia contradicted his wife's account of the attack in their room, both Lorlando and Frank Jordano were tried for murder. Frank received the death sentence; his father was sentenced to life in prison. However, nine months later, Rosie told a reporter for the *Times-Picayne* that she wanted to retract her testimony because St. Joseph had appeared to her

Victims of the New Orleans axe murders were treated at Charity Hospital between 1918 and 1919. *Wikimedia Commons.*

in a dream and told her the truth: she had been pressured into identifying the Jordanos. In December 1920, Lorlando and Frank Jordano were set free.

On March 14, 1919, the *New Orleans Times-Picayune* received a letter to the editor that was signed "The Axeman." In the letter, the writer said that he could have committed a murder every night if he wanted to. He closed his letter by making a "proposition" to the readers: "I am very fond of Jazz Music, and I swear by all the devils in the nether regions that every person shall be spared in whose home a jazz band is in full swing on Tuesday at 12:15 a.m." Anyone who did not play a jazz record on their record players at that time would "get the axe."

On August 10, 1919, a grocer named Steve Boca was awakened by the appearance of a man standing over his bed with an axe. Boca told the police that the man struck him with the axe and knocked him unconscious. After a few minutes, Boca regained consciousness. He could tell by the blood pouring down his face that he had been struck in the head. Boca ran to the house of his neighbor Frank Genusa. Before Boca could say very much, he passed out on the floor. After Boca was treated for his wound, he fully recovered but could not recall the details of his attack. The police walked through Boca's house and discovered a familiar pattern: a panel in the back door of the home had been chiseled out. Once again, nothing of value had been removed.

The Axeman's next victim was not connected to the grocery business in any way. On September 3, 1919, several neighbors knocked on the door of nineteen-year-old Sarah Laumann, who lived alone. When she did not answer, they broke down the door. They found her lying on the bed. She had been knocked out by a blow to the head with a blunt object. A bloody axe was found on the lawn. Apparently, the intruder had entered through a window. She suffered a severe head wound and the loss of several teeth, but she eventually recovered. Like Steve Boca, she was unable to remember any details.

The Axeman's final murder, that of Mike Pepitone, a grocer, took place on the night of October 27, 1919. Pepitone's wife was awakened by the sounds of fighting coming from the next room. She became alarmed because her husband slept in that room. As she opened the door, she caught a glimpse of a large man slipping out of the room through a door on the opposite side. Her greatest fears were realized when she saw her husband's bloody body lying on the bed. His assailant had struck him in the head several times with an axe. Blood covered the room, including a painting of the Virgin Mary. The distraught woman was unable to recall any features of the shadowy man she had seen exiting her husband's bedroom. The police who investigated the crime believed that it would be just a matter of time before the Axeman struck again, totally unaware that this was his last murder.

It turned out, however, that this was not the conclusion of the Mike Pepitone murder case. On the afternoon of December 2, 1920, a former

New Orleans resident named Joseph Mumfre was strolling down the street when a heavily "veiled" woman stepped out of a doorway and emptied her revolver into his body. The last person Mumfre saw as he lay dying on the sidewalk was his murderer. When the police arrived, the woman was still standing over her victim's body, holding the murder weapon. Several days after she was arrested, she told the police that her name was Esther Albano and that she was the widow of Mike Pepitone. She admitted that she had lied to the police after her husband died. She actually did see his murderer as he ran away, and she knew who he was. When Mumfre lived in New Orleans, he blackmailed many of the Italian residents of the city. He was imprisoned in 1911, right after the first axe murders. The Axeman was dormant in the same years that Mumfre was in prison, but after he was released, the serial killer started up again. This circumstantial evidence was not strong enough to connect Mumfre to the Axeman, however. Mumfre's murderer was tried in court in Los Angeles and found guilty of murder. Mrs. Pepitone was sentenced to ten years in prison, but she served only three years. She disappeared from history following her release from prison.

A number of theories have been offered to explain the Axeman's motivation for committing the murders. Some residents of New Orleans suspected that the Black Hand (i.e., the mafia) was behind most of the murders. However, historians have rejected this theory because most mafia killers would have left no survivors alive at all. Another theory holds that the murderer was a sadist who targeted women as a rule. Men were murdered if they interfered with the assassin's attempt to get to the women in their house. Another criminologist posited that the killer was a psychopath in the Jack the Ripper mold. The most far-fetched theory suggests that the Axeman's primary intention was to make jazz more popular.

Something good did emerge from this bloody episode from New Orleans's history. A composer named Joseph John Davilla said that he wrote "The Mysterious Axeman's Jazz (Don't Scare Me Papa)" while waiting for the Axeman. He offered his sheet music for sale on March 20, only two days after many people in New Orleans played jazz music to avoid becoming the Axeman's next victim. Many people at the time believed that Davilla wrote the letter himself to promote his song. This allegation has never been proven to be true.

BONNIE AND CLYDE'S FATAL VISIT TO LOUISIANA

The phrase "us against the world" has long inspired the titles of songs and movies. For generations, the words have resonated with young lovers whose parents disapprove of their relationship. For young married couples beset by mounting bills, sickness and unforeseen calamities, the phrase has acquired an even broader meaning. In the 1930s, the embodiment of "us against the world" for many people was found in Bonnie Parker and Clyde Barrow, whose relatively short criminal career provided the media with months of sensationalist stories. However, by the time the couple met their bloody end in Louisiana, it had become clear that these "misunderstood lovers" were actually just a pair of cold-blooded killers.

Bonnie and Clyde's background was fairly typical for thousands of young people who have grown up poor and restless in small, rural Texas towns. Clyde Barrow was born in 1909 to parents who eked out a living for themselves and their growing family on a farm. In the early 1920s, Clyde, his parents and his six siblings moved to the "big city" in search of a better life. Instead, they found themselves living in a tenant building in a slum in West Dallas. Before Clyde's parents could afford a tent, they lived underneath their car for several months. As a teenager, Clyde found himself on the wrong side of the law. When he was seventeen, he was arrested for failing to return a rented car. Not long thereafter, Clyde was arrested again, this time for stealing turkeys with his brother Buck. Between 1927 and 1929, Clyde fluctuated between working legitimate jobs and robbing money from safes and stores and stealing cars.

Bonnie Parker and Clyde Barrow became infamous for a string of murders and robberies that they committed between 1932 and 1934. *Wikimedia Commons.*

Bonnie Parker's life growing up was also a struggle, although not to the same extent that Clyde's life was. She was born in Rowena, Texas, in 1910. Her father, Charles Robert Parker, was a bricklayer who died in 1914, when Bonnie was only four years old. Following her husband's death, Bonnie's mother, Emma (Krause) Parker, moved Bonnie and her three other children back to Cement City, a suburb of West Dallas. Emma supported herself and her family by working as a seamstress. As a sophomore in high school, Bonnie became romantically involved with Roy Thornton, who did not live up to her dreams of the ideal husband. He left home for extended periods and was jailed for breaking the law on several occasions. In January 1929, Bonnie decided that she had had enough.

Bonnie moved back home to live with her mother and supported herself by working as a waitress in Dallas. In the diary Bonnie kept at this time, she wrote poetry and expressed her longing for a better life.

Bonnie Parker's rather mundane life changed forever on January 20, 1930, when she was nineteen years old. She was unemployed and staying with a girlfriend while recovering from a broken arm when Clyde Barrow knocked on the door. Bonnie, who was making hot chocolate with her friend, was immediately attracted to the bold stranger. Over the next few weeks, the couple's mutual attraction blossomed into a genuine romantic relationship. Later that year, their love affair was temporarily interrupted when Clyde was convicted of auto theft and incarcerated at the Eastham Prison Farm on April 30. Using a gun that Bonnie had smuggled into the prison, Clyde escaped for a short period before he was apprehended and returned to prison. Throughout the duration of his prison sentence, Clyde was sexually assaulted multiple times. He killed one of the men who molested him, but he was never charged with the crime because a friend of his who was serving a life sentence took the blame.

Clyde was paroled on February 2, 1932, thanks in large part to his mother's letter-writing. Once he was free, Clyde picked up where he had left off before he was sent to prison, robbing small businesses like gas stations and grocery stores so that he and his gang could attack Eastham Prison Farm as retribution for the abuse that he endured there. His "gang" consisted primarily of Bonnie Parker and Guy Fults. By this time, Clyde was using a Browning automatic rifle (BAR) in his robberies. On April 19, 1932, Bonnie and Guy were captured while trying to steal weapons from a hardware store. Bonnie served only a few months in jail before she was released because of a hung jury. Guy Fults did not fare nearly as well as Bonnie. He was tried and convicted of attempted robbery and sentenced to serve time in prison. Following his release from prison, Fults had no interest in rejoining the Barrow Gang.

Soon, murder was added to the number of crimes Clyde Barrow was committing. On April 30, 1932, Clyde was the getaway driver for the robbery of a store in Hillsboro, Texas. During the robbery, the owner of the store, J.N. Bucher, was killed. Then in August 1932, Clyde and two members of his gang, Ross Dyer and Raymond Hamilton, were at a dance, drinking moonshine whiskey in the parking lot, when Sheriff C.G. Maxwell and Deputy Eugene C. Moore walked up to them. Concerned that they were about to be arrested for the murder of the store owner in the Hillsboro robbery, Clyde and Hamilton pulled out their pistols and started firing, killing the deputy and wounding the sheriff. Maxwell was the first of eight law enforcement officers to be killed by Clyde Barrow and his gang.

On Christmas Eve 1932, a sixteen-year-old boy named W.D. Jones became the newest addition to the Barrow Gang. Because Jones had known the Barrow family since he was a child, Barrow knew that he could be trusted. On Christmas Day, Jones proved that he had what it took to be a member of the Barrow Gang by helping Burrow murder a young man named Doyle Johnson while they were attempting to steal his car. On January 6, 1933, Barrow shot Tarrant County deputy Malcolm Davis in the chest with a sixteen-gauge shotgun after the gang stumbled into a trap the police had set for someone else.

The composition of the Barrow Gang changed once again after W.D. Jones's brother Buck was released from prison with a complete pardon. Within just a few days, Buck and his wife, Blanche, traveled to Bonnie and Clyde's house in Joplin, Missouri, with the intention of persuading Clyde to give himself up. Buck and Blanche soon found themselves enmeshed in Bonnie and Clyde's devil-may-care lifestyle, drinking beer and playing cards late into the night. One night, after a bout of heavy drinking, Clyde accidentally fired his BAR while cleaning inside the house. The blast was so loud that one of his neighbors alerted the police. Thinking that the house was occupied by a nest of bootleggers, five members of the Joplin Police Department pulled up to the house in two police cars. As soon as Clyde and Buck saw the officers exit their cars, they opened fire, fatally wounding Constable J.W. Harryman and killing Detective Harry L. McGinnis. Bonnie fired a hail of bullets at the remaining officers as they took cover. Bonnie jumped into Clyde's car as it pulled out of the driveway. The gang slowed down only long enough to grab Blanche, who was chasing her runaway dog, and pull her into the car. Back at the station, the officers reported that one of the buttons on Clyde's suit fell off, and one of the bullets from their guns ricocheted off the wall and grazed Buck.

When the officers investigated the Barrow Gang's hideout, they discovered a treasure trove of artifacts left behind by Bonnie and Clyde in their hurry to escape, including rolls of undeveloped camera film. The police developed the film in the darkroom of the *Joplin Globe* and were amazed to find posed photographs the couple had taken of each other smoking cigars and brandishing firearms. When the *Joplin Globe* sent the photographs over the newswire, Bonnie and Clyde were transformed into overnight celebrities. To someone unfamiliar with the pair's criminal history, they appeared to be just a couple of young lovers who enjoyed each other's company and driving free and easy down the highway. Their legend grew by leaps and bounds over the next few months when it became clear that, in some ways, they were amateurs at bank robbing. Their failed attempt at robbing the bank in Lucerne, Indiana, was followed by their successful robbery in Okabena, Minnesota. In Ralston, Louisiana, the couple tried to steal a car owned by Dillard Darby but ended up kidnapping Darby and Sophia Stone. They repeated this pattern of kidnapping robbery victims and police officers several times between 1932 and 1934. Their Robin Hood–like image grew out of their habit of giving their victims money before releasing them. Many people who were enamored with Bonnie and Clyde's carefree lifestyle chose to ignore tales of the murders they had committed when it was more convenient than taking their victims hostage. Before long, though, it would become difficult to view Bonnie and Clyde as anything but heartless killers.

Bonnie and Clyde soon discovered that they were paying for their newfound notoriety with the loss of their privacy. They had to be more careful when driving through small towns or buying groceries for fear of being recognized. Instead of taking baths in a cast-iron bathtub in a motel or eating at a restaurant, they were forced to bathe in creeks and ponds and to cook over an open fire in a secluded area. Their tempers were exacerbated by the stress of having to squeeze their entire gang into one car and drive mile after endless mile. Predictably, arguments broke out between the gang members. Fed up with the constant quarreling, Jones left the gang for a few months but returned on June 8.

That same month, Bonnie was severely injured when Clyde flipped their car in a ravine in Wellington, Texas. Bonnie's right leg was severely burned, either from burning gasoline or battery acid that splashed on her leg during the wreck. Later, Jones told authorities that the third-degree burns on Bonnie's leg had removed much of her skin, exposing white patches of bone. For a while, she appeared to be near death. Bonnie was in so much pain over the next few weeks that she was unable to walk. When Bonnie tired of hopping around on one foot, Barrow had to pick her up and carry her around. Bonnie got some relief from a farm family who treated her injury, but her recovery time was cut short after the gang kidnapped County Sheriff George Cory and City Marshal Paul Hardy in Erick, Oklahoma, and tied them to a tree with barbed wire after handcuffing them. Bonnie, Clyde, Buck and Blanche hid out in a tourist court in Fort Smith, Arkansas, to give Bonnie's leg time to heal, but their stay was short-lived after Buck and Jones killed Town Marshal Henry D. Humphrey in a botched robbery attempt. As soon as Bonnie's leg was hastily treated and wrapped up, the gang hit the road once again.

The five members of the Barrow Gang barreled down the highway until they finally decided to spend the night at the Red Crown Tourist Court just south of Platte City, Missouri. They decided to rent two cabins at the cost of four dollars each. To protect their privacy, they covered the windows with newspapers. Instead of going out to eat together, they ordered five meals at the same time to reduce the amount of time they spent out in public. Despite the need to "lay low," Blanche went to the local drugstore to buy medical supplies like atropine sulfate for Bonnie's leg. At the time, she was wearing jodhpur riding breeches, a type of attire that was rarely seen in Missouri. Having been alerted by the sheriff's departments in Oklahoma, Texas and Arkansas to be on the lookout for any strangers buying medical supplies, Sheriff Holt Coffey went into action when he heard about the attractive woman wearing jodhpur riding breeches in the drugstore. After finding out where the woman was staying, the sheriff assembled a collection of law enforcement officers, armed with two Thompson submachine guns, an iron shield and an armored car that he borrowed from the sheriff in Kansas City. At 11:00 p.m., Coffey knocked on the back door of Blanche's and Buck's cabin. He announced that he wanted to speak to someone inside the cabin. Blanche told him that she needed time to get dressed. The sound of their voices carried over to the cabin next door, waking Clyde. When he peered through the window and saw the armored car and Coffey carrying the shield, he grabbed his BAR and began spraying the men with bullets. He had stolen the miliary-grade weapon from the national guard armory in Enid, Oklahoma. The rounds penetrated the so-called armor of the armored car, striking the driver in both legs. The deputy inside the car put it in reverse. As the car backed away from the cabins, the deputy and other officers started firing bullets from their two machine guns at the cabin, but both guns jammed after a minute or so. During the gunfight, two of the bullets hit Sheriff Coffey's nineteen-year-old son, who was watching the excitement from the nearby tavern. He was saved by a waitress, who pulled him inside. While Clyde was opening the door of the garage where the gang's car was hidden, Bonnie and W.D. Jones grabbed handfuls of personal belongings and jumped inside the car. As Clyde opened the garage door for Blanche and Buck, a bullet struck Buck in the left side of his head. Frantically, Blanche and Clyde pulled out of the garage, barely missing the car that had been parked there to block their exit. In the hail of bullets that shattered the car's windows, Blanche was hit in the eye by glass fragments and was nearly blinded, and Bonnie's burn wound reopened. Knowing that their guns were no match for Clyde's BAR, Coffey's officers decided not to give pursuit. As the car careened out of the Red Crown Tourist Court, the gang left behind two bullet-ridden cabins, the bullet holes in the front bearing mute witness to the gunfight.

The Barrow Gang drove the ten miles to the outskirts of Kansas City more slowly than they would have preferred because Clyde had to stop periodically to fix the tires. Blanche held Buck's head in her lap. Part of his bleeding brain was visible through the gaping hole in his head. Both Blanche and Buck were soaked in blood. As the sun rose in the sky on the morning of June 24, Clyde pulled the car into an abandoned amusement park called Dexfield Park in Dexter, Iowa. Clyde set up camp in the sweltering ninety-degree heat. Thinking that the bullet holes in their vehicle would attract attention, Clyde and W.D. stole a car and bought men's pants and shirts at John Love's store, gauze and antiseptic at the drugstore and five meals at the local restaurant. By the time Clyde had returned to camp, the store owners were exchanging stories about their encounters with the polite stranger. A farmer passing by the car noticed bloodstained bandages and clothes. Before long, over one hundred local officers, including police officers from Des Moines, had gathered around the gang's campsite. While Clyde was cooking hot dogs over a campfire, Bonnie saw a group of men about one hundred yards away heading in their direction. Clyde grabbed his BAR and began shooting into the trees, dropping limbs and branches on the approaching lawmen. As W.D. stood up, he was hit in the chest with buckshot. Clyde yelled, "Get in the car!" W.D. was struck again as he climbed inside. While Bonnie, Blanche and Buck scrambled to get in the car, Clyde fired a barrage at the lawmen. Taking a bullet in the shoulder, Clyde moved the car forward until he reached an obstacle, and then he put it reverse. At that moment, another bullet hit Clyde in the shoulder. Unable to see clearly, Clyde backed the car over a stump and got stuck. In desperation, the gang members took off through the woods on foot. Buck was shot again, this time in the back. Bonnie took two pellets to the stomach. Clyde grabbed Buck and Blanche by the arms and pulled them through the brush while W.D. carried Bonnie, in spite of his injuries. They all made it as far as a fence. Then while Bonnie, W.D. and Clyde worked their way up the hill, Buck and Blanche lay on the ground, unable to go any farther. Bonnie, W.D. and Clyde continued until they reached a river. Clyde attempted to run over to the bridge and try to steal a car somewhere nearby, but it was surrounded by policemen. He fired his BAR, but the pain in his shoulder prevented him from hitting anyone. One of the lawmen fired back, knocking the BAR out of Clyde's hands and grazing his cheek. Clyde hurried over to W.D., who was standing by the edge of the river. With Bonnie clinging to his back, W.D. followed Clyde across the river. Hoping to escape detection by the pursuing lawmen, they entered a cornfield. When Clyde emerged from the other side, he was met by a farmer and his son. Clyde informed them that he was not going to hurt them; he just needed their car. As soon as the farmer nodded yes, Clyde whistled, and W.D. and Bonnie came out of the cornfield. After gently helping Bonnie into the back seat. Clyde and W.D. climbed into the front seat of the farmer's Plymouth and took off. It was 6:00 a.m.

Blanche and Buck did not fare nearly as well as the rest of their family. After Clyde, W.D. and Bonnie disappeared over the hill, some of the officers decided to check the underbrush not far from the car. A national guardsman who worked full time as a dentist walked over to a fallen tree where Blanche and Buck had taken cover and was surprised to find himself staring down the barrel of Buck's pistol. His instincts took over, and he fired before Buck could shoot, hitting him in the shoulder. When the smoke cleared, Blanche rushed over to Buck's side. He assured her that he was OK, even though he had been shot in the back, shoulder and chest, and brain matter was beginning to ooze from the hole in his skull. Buck was transported to Kings

Daughters Hospital in Perry, Iowa, where he died five days later on July 29. His mother, Cumie Barrow, was at his bedside. Even before the lawmen left the scene, souvenir hunters removed much of the evidence, digging bullets out of logs and trees.

Meanwhile, the heat was rising for the surviving members of the Barrow Gang. Aerial surveillance and on-the-ground investigations of abandoned buildings and backroads turned up nothing. In fact, some people believed that the infamous couple had succumbed to their wounds because nothing was heard from them for several weeks. In actuality, Bonnie and Clyde had decided to camp out in various places until they recovered from their wounds. After stealing three BARs, pistols and ammunition from an armory in Plattville, Illinois, on August 20, Clyde and W.D. decided to go to Mississippi, where W.D. announced that he was leaving the gang after eight months because running with them was filled with more misery than excitement. Now that the size of the Barrow Gang was down to only two members, Bonnie and Clyde were reduced to stealing blankets, pillows and clothes from stores and private homes. Sensing that the end was near, the pair decided to visit their families one last time. To avoid being recognized, Bonnie dyed her naturally blond hair, and Clyde wore a wig. A couple of times, Bonnie dressed Clyde up like a woman and put lipstick on him. W.D. had the same idea and traveled to Houston to see his mother. However, the police suspected that W.D. might show up there sometime and arrested him on November 16.

Surprisingly, the Dallas Police Department did not stake out the homes of the Barrow Gang's families. Some people believed that the Dallas police feared encountering one of the most ruthless criminals in America without backup. In November, the police proved that they were not ignoring Bonnie and Clyde when they arrested W.D. Jones in Houston. Under questioning, Jones gave a few answers that seemed to veer from the truth. For example, W.D. claimed that when he was seventeen years old, Bonnie and Clyde forced him to join their gang. He did, however, give a complete rundown of the gang's gun battles with the law—none of which, W.D. claimed, he fired a gun in—over the previous eight months. Sheriff Schmid kept W.D.'s arrest out of the media in the hopes that Clyde would never find out about it.

Sheriff Schmid got a break when he learned that Bonnie and Clyde were going to meet family members on an isolated road near Sowers, Texas, to celebrate Cumie Barrow's birthday. Several hours before Bonnie and Clyde's arrival, Sheriff Schmid and three deputies, Bob Alcorn, Ted Hinton and Ed Caster, parked their car out of sight and hid in a ditch seventy-five yards off the road. The men were armed with a BAR, two Thompson submachine guns and a repeating rifle. As the sun began to slip below the horizon, a car pulled up. Inside were Marie Barrow (Clyde's sister), the driver, Joe Bill (Marie's boyfriend) and members of the Barrow and Parker families. When a second car drove down the road a few minutes later and parked alongside the first car, Joe Bill flashed the headlights. Suddenly, they opened fire; the windshield of Clyde's car exploded in a cloud of shattered glass. Immediately, the passengers in the car hit the floor. Clyde returned fire and gunned his engine. When the dust finally cleared, Bonnie and Clyde were gone. Once again, they had slipped out of the grasp of the law. To deflect attention from the Barrow Gang's escape, Sheriff Schmid told reporters that W.D. Jones had been arrested and that he had confessed.

The Barrow Gang fled Texas and headed for one of their hiding places in Oklahoma, where they could "lick their wounds." They were able to find both a doctor and a nurse, who treated Bonnie and Clyde for bullet wounds in their knees and legs. While Clyde and Bonnie were recuperating, Clyde's hatred of law enforcement reached the boiling point. By the time Bonnie and Clyde were on the road again, Clyde was ready to commit his most daring breach of the law. Former Barrow Gang member Raymond Hamilton, who was serving time at Texas Eastham Farm, persuaded an about-to-be-paroled former drug addict, Henry Methvin, to help him get out of prison in exchange for $2,000. After James Mullins, a hired hand, was paroled on January 10, 1934, he met up with Raymond's brother Floyd. The two men then had a meeting with Clyde in a secluded spot west of Dallas, where they came up with a plan to free Raymond. On January 13, Floyd and Raymond sneaked into Eastham and crept under a bridge, where they stashed an innertube containing two .45-caliber pistols and ammunition. On Sunday morning, Floyd and his wife visited Raymond in prison and told him about the escape plan. On January 16, Raymond and his friend Joe Palmer were stacking wood and cutting brush as part of a work crew. One of the squad guards, Major Crowson, noticed Raymond and Joe's strange behavior. All of a sudden, Joe shot Crowson in the stomach and another guard, Olin Bozeman, in the hip. Amid the confusion caused by the gunfire, Raymond, Joe and two other prisoners ran into a ditch. Clyde and Mullins, who were waiting in their car, fired their rifles into the trees when they saw the escapees coming. Clyde zig-zagged across fields and sped down dirt and gravel roads to avoid police roadblocks. The next morning, newspapers across the country reported on the daring jailbreak with totally inaccurate details, most of which exaggerated Bonnie's role. Meanwhile, Crowson and Bozeman were in the hospital, fighting for their lives. Before Crowson died from the bullet wound in his abdomen on January 27, Prison Chief Lee Simons promised him that everyone who took part in the jailbreak would be tracked down and killed.

Following the Eastham breakout, apprehending the culprits became the top priority for the Texas Department of Corrections. Prison Boss Simmons interviewed three Texas Rangers for the job of bringing Bonnie and Clyde to justice, dead or alive. Retired Texas Ranger Frank Hamer was his first choice for a couple of reasons. First of all, in his twenty years in law enforcement, Hamer had killed fifty-three criminals; he himself was wounded seventeen times. He was also Simmons's first choice because, unlike the other two candidates, Hamer had no qualms about killing a woman. He began tailing Bonnie and Clyde on February 10, going so far as to sleep in his car to make sure that his quarry did not get too far away from him. In just a few weeks, Hamer had become familiar with the highways used by Bonnie and Clyde. He also kept tabs on the gang's Black Lake hideout.

The glamorous image of Bonnie and Clyde as a couple of "wild and crazy kids" was changed forever on April 1 (Easter Sunday). Two highway patrolmen, H.D. Murphy and Edward Bryant, were driving along Route 114 on their motorcycles when they spotted a car parked on Dove Road, not far from Grapevine, Texas. The officers assumed that the driver and passengers were in need of roadside assistance and stopped. Two members of the Barrow Gang, Clyde and either Methvin or Bonnie, fired a shotgun and a pistol, killing both patrolmen. Testimony from an eyewitness who claimed that Bonnie killed both officers received national attention in the newspapers. Later, Methvin took the credit for firing the first shot at Bryant; then Clyde shot and killed Murphy. The senseless murders created a firestorm in the media, completely reversing public opinion on Bonnie and Clyde. In the weeks following the Grapevine killings, Highway Patrol Boss L.G. Phares offered a reward of $1,000 for the "dead bodies" of the murderers. Shortly thereafter, Governor Amanda "Ma" Ferguson offered a $500 reward for the capture of both Bonnie and Clyde, mostly because most people believed that Bonnie was Murphy's killer.

The Barrow Gang's reputation was damaged even more after Clyde and Methvin killed a sixty-year-old constable named William "Cal" Campbell not far from Commerce, Oklahoma. While they were in Commerce, Clyde and Methvin abducted Police Chief Percy Boy after crossing the state line in Kansas. Before the Barrow Gang released their captive, they gave him a little money and a clean shirt. Before they drove off, Bonnie told him that she didn't smoke cigars, referencing the published photographs of her smoking a cigar. Her parting words did little to counter the public's perception of her as a heartless killer, an image that was largely generated by the media after the Grapevine murders.

By the spring of 1934, Bonnie and Clyde were nearing the end of their wild and crazy ride to infamy. Four states were now charging Clyde with sixteen counts of robbery, auto theft, escape and murder. In May, Methvin was beginning to feel that he needed to break off from the Barrow Gang. On May 22, Clyde drove Henry to a café and instructed him to buy some sandwiches. While Henry was ordering, he noticed Clyde drive off. Assuming that Clyde had been "spooked" by a passing police car, Henry walked out of the café, stole a car and drove to his brother's house. Clyde and Bonnie went to Henry's parents' house to find out where he went. Methvin's mother told them that they didn't know where he was but that he would probably return home the next morning. After Bonnie and Clyde left Henry's house, his mother, Ivy Methvin, notified Sheriff Jordan that Bonnie and Clyde were coming back the next morning to pick up Henry.

When Frank Hamer found out that Bonnie and Clyde were going to visit Methvin's family in Bienville Parish, he gathered his posse, consisting of Manny Gault, Bob Alcorn, Ted Hinton, Sheriff Jordan and his deputy, Prentiss Oakely. They decided to conceal themselves in a bushy area along the road leading to the Methvins' property at dawn. Before long, Henry Methvin joined the group. Sheriff Jordan suggested that they jack up a truck owned by Henry's father near their hiding place in the hopes that when Clyde saw the truck, he would pull over and stop, thinking that Henry's father needed assistance. They ended up waiting in the bushes all day and night. At sunrise on May 23, they were ready to give up and leave. Then at 9:15 a.m., their patience was rewarded. The men could see Clyde's Ford V8 racing down the road in their direction. Predictably, he slowed down when he saw Ivy Methvin standing by the apparently disabled truck parked on the roadside. Oakley fired first, hitting Clyde in front of his left ear and killing him instantly. Then the rest of the officers began shooting at the same time as the car slowly moved forward and came to rest in a ditch. The blast from the guns was so loud that all of the deputies were deaf for a short time. Ivy Methvin ran down the road as soon as the shooting ended. With movie camera in hand, Ted Hinton filmed the 112 bullet holes on the outside of the car, the weapons inside the car and Bonnie and Clyde's bullet-ridden corpses. Clyde's upper torso hung halfway out the widow; Bonnie's head was between her legs. Part of Bonnie's right hand and half of Clyde's head had been blown away. A half-eaten sandwich was still clutched in Bonnie's left

This handmade marker was erected at the site of Bonnie and Clyde's ambush. *Wikimedia Commons.*

hand. The interior of the car was covered with blood and bits of flesh. The weapons inside the car included shotguns, automatic rifles, several different pistols and boxes of bullets. Each member of the posse received $200.23 in reward money for taking down America's most wanted criminals. Virtually everyone in America who had been following the thrilling tale of Bonnie and Clyde fully expected it to end in blazing gunfire and bloody death, including Bonnie, who wrote in her poem "Trail's End":

> *They have been shot at before,*
> *But they do not ignore*
> *That death is the wages of sin.*

The posse arranged for the death car, with Bonnie and Clyde's bodies still inside, to be towed to the Conger Furniture Store and Funeral Home in Arcadia, Louisiana. The undertaker complained that he had difficulty embalming Bonnie and Clyde because the embalming fluid kept leaking out of their bodies. Within a matter of a few hours, around twelve thousand people descended on the little town in the hopes of catching a glimpse of the bodies of Bonnie and Clyde. Even though Bonnie and Clyde had wanted to be buried together, Bonnie's family wanted her to be interred in a separate graveyard. Approximately twenty thousand people attended Bonnie's funeral. She was originally laid to rest in Fishtrap Cemetery, but her body was exhumed in 1945 and reburied in Crown Hill Cemetery in Dallas. Clyde was buried next to his brother Buck in Western Heights Cemetery in Dallas. Bonnie and Clyde's death car enjoyed a sort of second life after the ambush. Ruth Warren, the original owner of the vehicle, reclaimed the death car from Sheriff Jordan in August 1934. When she finally took possession of the car, the interior was still plastered with bloodstains, human tissue and even a few human teeth. The car was exhibited throughout the country at flea markets, county fairs and amusement parks for around forty years. It was then purchased by Whiskey Pete's Hotel and Casino in Primm, Nevada, where it is now on permanent display.

Not surprisingly, the saga of Bonnie and Clyde has been transferred to the big screen a number of times. The first film adaptation of Bonnie and Clyde story, 1958's *The Bonnie Parker Story*, starred Dorothy Provine as Bonnie and Jack Hogan as "Guy" Barrow. Arthur Penn's groundbreaking 1967 film, *Bonnie and Clyde*, starring Faye Dunaway as Bonnie and Warren Beatty as Clyde, depicted both the romantic and brutal aspects of the couple's lives while taking liberties with historical fact, especially in its depiction of Texas Ranger Frank Hamer. The made-for-TV movie *Bonnie & Clyde: The True Story* is much less gruesome than its 1967 predecessor. *Bonnie and Clyde Italian Style* (1983) is a comedy about a dim-witted young couple who are forced to commit a rash of crimes in the streets of Italy. *The Other Side of Bonnie and Clyde* (1968) is a docudrama that includes never-before-seen footage of the couple's bullet-ridden corpses inside their car. *Bonnie and Clyde: The True Story* (1992), starring Tracey Needham and Gary Hoffman, is considered one of the best cinematic depictions of the murderous duo. It was shot on location at some of the actual crime scenes associated with the couple in Texas. Probably the most bizarre adaptation of Bonnie and Clyde's story is *Bonnie and Clyde vs. Dracula* (2008), in which the pair encounters the reanimated vampire. A straight-to-video version titled *Bonnie & Clyde Justified* (2014)

A replica of Bonnie and Clyde's death car can be found in the Hollywood Car Museum. *Wikimedia Commons.*

attempts to recreate the period but falls short of its goal because of its limited budget. The film stars Ashley Hayes as Bonnie and Jim Poole as Clyde. *The Highwaymen* (2019) tells the story of Texas Ranger Frank Hamer's pursuit of Bonnie and Clyde in 1934. It stars Kevin Costner and Woody Harrelson. Critics praised the film for being much more realistic than the 1967 film.

Even before the release of *The Bonnie Parker Story* in 1958, the two bandits had served as the inspiration for crime films. *They Live by Night* (1949) chronicles the adventures of young lovers Farley Granger and Cathy O'Donnell, who become fugitives from the law. *Gun Crazy* (1950) stars Peggy Cummins and John Dall. In this tale, Bonnie is a femme fatale who talks her lover into joining her in a life of crime. Terrence Malick's *Badlands* (1973) is based on the killing spree of a Bonnie and Clyde–like couple, Charles Starkweather and Caril Ann Fugate, in the 1950s. Robert Altman's *Thieves Like Us* (1974), which is essentially a remake of *They Live by Night*, is about a young escapee from a prison camp (Keith Carradine) who falls in with a poor, uneducated girl in Mississippi in the 1930s. *Tir a vue* (1984) chronicles the adventure of a couple (Sandrine Bonnaire and Laurent Malet) who commit robberies and murders throughout France. Told from a contemporary viewpoint, *Teenage Bonnie and Klepto Clyde* (1993) is the story of a nerdy young man (Scott Wolf) who works in a burger joint and a street gang member (Maureen Flannigan) who cut loose and go on a killing spree. Oliver Stone's *Natural Born Killers* (1994) satirizes America's love affair with outlaws. The story, written by Quentin Tarantino, follows the bloody trail of a young couple (Woody Harrelson and Juliette Lewis) who kill more than fifty people on their honeymoon. *The End* (2007) follows the criminal activities of an older couple (Jeremy Thomas and Ella May) who act on their dream of taking an entirely new path in life and becoming entirely different people. In the film *Ain't Them Bodies Saints* (2013), Ruth (Rooney Mara) and Bob (Casey Affleck) are a young couple who engage in criminal behavior. After they are caught, Bob takes full blame for their crimes and is sent to prison. He returns home to discover that Ruth had a baby while he was gone. In *Scavenger Killers* (2014), a suave judge (Robert T. Bogue) and an attractive defense attorney (Rachael Robbins) explore life on the other side of the law, killing anyone who gets in their way. *Queen and Slim* (2019) puts an entirely new slant on the Bonnie and Clyde trope. In this version of the story, a young Black couple run for their lives after a racist white police officer is shot and killed during a routine traffic stop.

Not surprisingly, a museum has been established to capitalize on the influx of tourists who still flock to Louisiana to experience Bonnie and Clyde's death site firsthand. The Bonnie & Clyde Ambush Museum is located in Gibsland, Louisiana, off Highway 154. The museum occupies Ma Canfield's restaurant, where Bonnie had just bought a ham sandwich just before she and Clyde were gunned down seven miles away. The founder of the museum was L.J. "Boots" Hinton, who was born the same year Bonnie and Clyde died. His father, Deputy Sheriff Ted Hinton, was part of the six-man posse who bushwhacked the outlaws. Hinton recalled that Bonnie Parker served him meals when she worked as a waitress at Marco's Café in Dallas, Texas. At the time, he had no idea that this polite young woman would become one of the subjects of a nationwide manhunt. When Hinton's poor health forced him to retire, another man who loved everything connected to Bonnie and Clyde, Percy Carver, became the curator. Carver first saw the couple's death car in 1942, when Ted Toddy bought the car for $13,500 and put it on display. Carver remembers looking inside the car's window and seeing a tooth and pieces of bone. After reading about the pair's exploits in an article published in *Guns and Gunfighters* magazine, Carver became a passionate collector of Bonnie and Clyde memorabilia, including three of Clyde

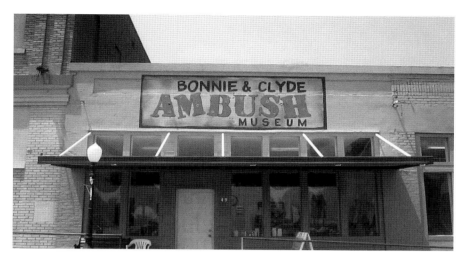

Artifacts pertaining to Bonnie and Clyde's death can be found at the Bonnie and Clyde Ambush Museum in Gibsland, Louisiana, off Highway 154. *Wikimedia Commons.*

Barrow's saxophones and a number of his guns, as well as the guns used by the members of the posse on that fateful day in May. Much of Carver's historical knowledge of Bonnie and Clyde comes from interviews he has conducted with their relatives, law enforcement officers and historians. Next to the museum is an authentic re-creation of Ma Canfield's restaurant. On May 23 (or the weekend closest to this date), a Bonnie and Clyde festival is held, during which volunteers reenact the ambush.

DR. CARL WEISS

DID HE ASSASSINATE GOVERNOR HUEY LONG?

Huey Long is generally regarded as one of the most charismatic of America's radical populist politicians. One of nine children, Huey Long was born in a "comfortable" farmhouse near Winnfield, Louisiana, although he frequently told potential voters that he was born in a log cabin. Although he was awarded a full scholarship to Louisiana State University, Long was unable to attend the university because his parents could not afford the textbooks. In 1914, he attended Tulane University Law School, learning enough after two semesters to pass the bar exam.

After establishing a private practice in Winnfield, Long entered the world of politics. He placed third in Louisiana's 1925 gubernatorial campaign but was elected governor of Louisiana in 1928, serving until 1932. Following an unsuccessful attempt by Long's political enemies to impeach him in 1929, Long focused on the upcoming Senate race, using a nickname "borrowed" from the *Amos and Andy* radio show: the Kingfish. After defeating Joseph E. Ransdell for a seat in the U.S. Senate, Long embarked on an ambitious public works program, building schools and a new state capitol. School enrollment increased by 20 percent because of his offer of free textbooks. In an attempt to realize his childhood dream of becoming president of the United States, Long publicly opposed President Roosevelt's New Deal policies, asserting that they did not do enough to help poor Americans in the current economic crisis. In February 1934, Long founded the Share the Wealth Plan, which he believed would get the country out of the Great Depression by offering benefits like free college tuition to veterans, federal

The slogan for Governor Huey Long's presidential campaign was "Every man a king." *Wikimedia Commons.*

aid to farmers and public works projects. The program would be funded by confiscating the wealth of the nation's richest people. By 1935, Long was actively running for president, hoping to displace President Roosevelt as the Democratic presidential candidate with political slogans like "Every man a king," taken from his February 23, 1934 radio address.

Huey Long's political ambitions came to a tragic end when one of his political opponents, Judge Benjamin Pavy, successfully thwarted Long's attempt to unseat him in St. Landry's Parrish. In 1933, one of the judge's daughters, Yvonne, married an ear, nose and throat doctor named Carl Weiss. In early September 1935, Weiss became outraged when he learned of a rumor, spread by Long, that Yvonne was part Black because her father, Benjamin Pavy, was a Black man. On September 8, 1935, Weiss decided to take revenge on Long for slandering his wife. Long was in the state capitol for a special session of the legislature, during which he planned to use gerrymandering to remove Pavy from his position. Weiss entered the newly built Louisiana State Capitol and waited behind a marble pillar just outside of the governor's office. As soon as Long left his office, accompanied by John Fournet and six bodyguards, Weiss drew a .32 automatic pistol and fired, hitting Long in the stomach. Just a few seconds later, the six bodyguards returned fire, killing Weiss. One of the bullets fired by the bodyguards ricocheted and hit Long in the lower spine. At first, Long's physician thought that his wounds were not serious; however, on further examination, he found that a bullet had severely injured one of Long's kidneys. Unfortunately, Long was too weak to survive another operation. To make matters worse, a team of special trauma physicians from New Orleans were held up by roadwork on the Airline Highway. Long succumbed to his wounds on September 10,

Left: History records that Huey Long was assassinated by Dr. Carl Weiss in the newly built state capitol on September 8, 1935. *Gracen Deerman*.

Below: Huey Long's towering tombstone stands at his burial site in Baton Rouge, Louisiana. *Wikimedia Commons*.

1935. Meanwhile, the coroner reported that Weiss's body was riddled with fifty-nine bullets. Over 200,000 mourners attended Long's funeral in Baton Rouge. He was buried on the grounds of the state capitol. Long's wife, Rose, who received thousands of letters of sympathy, filled her husband's position in the Senate.

The shadow of controversy still hovers over Huey Long's death. A retired criminal investigator for the U.S. Department of the Treasury is convinced that Dr. Carl Austin Weiss was not the murderer of Huey Long. Others, such as Francis Grevemberg, former superintendent of the Louisiana Department of State Police, hold firmly to the belief that Long was accidentally killed in the hail of bullets fired by his own bodyguards. Unless more evidence surfaces, Weiss remains the lone killer of Huey Long in the historical record.

TONI JO HENRY

THE ONLY WOMAN TO DIE IN LOUISIANA'S ELECTRIC CHAIR

Born in January 1916 near Shreveport, Louisiana, Annie Beatrice McQuiston was the third of five children. She was six years old when her mother died of tuberculosis. Her father, who began drinking heavily following his wife's death, remarried, but Toni Jo preferred living with her grandmother. When she was thirteen, Toni Jo began working in a macaroni factory, but she was fired when her boss learned that her mother had died of tuberculosis. Toni Jo's father beat her for losing her job; as a result, Toni Jo ran away from home. While living on the streets, she soon started using cocaine, smoking and drinking. By the time she was sixteen, Toni Jo had begun turning tricks in Shreveport to support her drug habit. By 1939, she was working in a brothel in Clarke County. She adopted a new name, Toni Jo Hood, which she believed was better suited for her profession.

Toni Jo had worked in the brothel for only a few weeks when she fell in love with one of her customers, a second-rate boxer named Claude "Cowboy" Henry. As their romance developed, Henry weaned Toni Jo off drugs by forcing her to go cold turkey. Before the couple was married, Henry neglected to tell Toni Jo that he was out on bail. When Toni Jo and Henry returned to Louisiana from their honeymoon in California, the police arrested Henry on a murder charge, bringing their marital bliss to an abrupt end. Prior to their marriage, Henry, who had a history of committing petty crimes, had beaten a San Antonio police officer named Arthur Sinclair to death in a Texas bar. Henry was tried and found guilty of the murder in January 1940. The court sentenced him to serve

Toni Jo White became the first woman to die in New Orleans's electric chair on March 23, 1943. *Gracen Deerman.*

fifty years in the Texas State Penitentiary in Huntsville, Texas.

Heartbroken at the prospect of having to live without her one true love, Toni Jo set about making plans to break her husband out of jail. The contacts she had made over the years got her in touch with an army deserter and ex-con named Harold "Arkie" Burkes. He claimed that because he had served time in Huntsville, he knew the layout of the prison. Actually, though, Arkie had no intention of helping Toni Jo. All he wanted was a ride to Arkansas. Toni Jo suggested that they pose as hitchhiking honeymooners so that they could steal the car of any good Samaritan who picked them up and whose clothes were approximately the same size as Henry's. On Valentine's Day 1940, a forty-one-year-old salesman named Joseph P. Calloway spied the pair walking along the roadside and asked them if they needed a ride. Toni Jo and Arkie thanked him and climbed inside his new 1940 Ford coupe, a fast and dependable vehicle that met their requirements for a getaway car. They had just passed through Jennings, Louisiana, when Arkie ordered Calloway to pull off the road. After robbing Calloway, the pair ordered him to climb into the trunk. As soon as they drove over to a paddock, Toni Jo and Arkie stopped the car and helped Calloway out of the trunk. They then ordered him to walk behind a haystack and strip. Once he was completely naked, they told him to kneel. Either Toni Jo or Arkie walked in front of Calloway and shot him between the eyes. They used one of the guns they had bribed a couple of juvenile delinquents to steal in Beaumont, Texas, a few days earlier. They gathered up Calloway's clothes so that Henry would have something to wear once he had broken out of prison.

After driving for three days, the couple spent the night in a seedy hotel. While Toni Jo was asleep, Arkie took the car and Calloway's clothes but left the .32-caliber pistol in the room. Needless to say, Toni Jo had a rude awakening the next morning when she realized that her partner in crime had taken Calloway's car and clothes. All she had left was the .32-caliber pistol and a sense of impending doom.

In desperation, Toni Jo decided to hide out in her aunt Emma's house in Shreveport. Toni Jo recounted her story about Calloway's murder to Aunt Emma. She, in turn, alerted her brother, who was a Louisiana state trooper. When Toni Jo was arrested shortly thereafter, she admitted to participating in Calloway's murder. She even told the Louisiana policeman where the body was buried. Toni Jo made it clear, though, that Arkie Burks was the one who had murdered Calloway. Police soon tracked down Arkie to his sister's house in Warren, Arkansas. Around the same time, Toni Jo was guiding investigators through the crime scene. She also gave them the murder weapon. Based on the information that Toni Jo and Arkie gave the police, they were both indicted for murder in the first degree.

Toni Jo was tried three times. Her first trial on March 22, 1940, was heavily covered in the *St. Charles Press* because of its sensationalistic elements. Not surprisingly, reporters focused on Toni Jo's good looks and sordid past. Despite her attempts to shift all of the blame on Arkie, the jury found Toni Jo guilty of murder and gave her the death penalty. However, Toni Jo's lawyers appealed against her sentence because of Judge Hood's prejudicial behavior during the proceedings. They won their appeal, and their client was granted another trial on February 3, 1942, with a new judge, Judge Pickerall. By trial's end, both Toni Jo and Arkie were found guilty and sentenced to die. Once again, however, Toni Jo's lawyers won her a new trial because of the prosecutor's improper questioning of prospective jurors during juror selection. Judge Pickerell presided over her third trial as well. The court found Toni Jo guilty a third time and sentenced her to die.

Toni Jo was sentenced to die in Louisiana's portable electric chair on November 28, 1942. Governor Sam Jones made it very clear that no more pleas for clemency would be accepted.

Shortly before her execution date, Toni Jo took full credit for Calloway's murder. Nevertheless, Toni Jo's accomplice was sent to the electric chair on March 23, 1943, primarily because he had not tried to prevent Toni Jo from killing Calloway. While awaiting her execution, Toni Jo was baptized a Catholic. After her head was shaved, she was allowed to wear a bandana. She was led to "Gruesome Gertie," the electric chair, and told to sit down. Just before the executioner, Grady Jarnett, said, "Goodbye, Toni Jo," she uttered a silent prayer. At exactly 12:05 p.m., Jarrett threw the switch that sent two thousand volts through Toni Jo's body. Two minutes later, the electricity was turned off. The doctors immediately examined Toni Jo's smoldering corpse and declared her dead.

Claude Henry's end was no less pathetic than those of Toni Jo and Arkie. Just four days before Toni Jo's execution, he escaped from prison in an attempt to see his wife one last time but was recaptured in Beaumont, Texas. He was paroled because of his heart disease just a few months later. On July 15, 1945, a café owner shot him to death.

MARK JAMES ROBERT ESSEX

THE NEW ORLEANS SNIPER

Mark James Robert Essex was born on August 12, 1949. He grew up in a religious family in Emporia, Kansas. His father worked as a foreman in a meatpacking plant, and his mother counseled disadvantaged preschool children. Essex's childhood can best be described as fairly typical for a boy with a middle-class upbringing at the time. He joined the Boy Scouts, played saxophone in the band and went hunting and fishing. Racism was not a very serious problem for Essex while he was living at home in the 1950s and 1960s. He dated girls of different races without any serious objections from his parents. In his early teens, Essex considered becoming a minister. However, while he was in high school, his interests gravitated toward the vocational fields. Following graduation, Essex attended Emporia State University for only one semester. With his father's urging, Essex decided to acquire vocational training while serving in the military, so he enlisted in the U.S. Navy in 1969 and immediately began his training as a dental technician. Later on, Essex claimed that he was subjected to racial slurs for two years. He said that he experienced even more bigotry while working as a bartender in an enlisted men's club, the Jolly Rotor, where some rooms were designated as being for "whites only." Essex had hoped the racism would cease after he was promoted to the rank of seaman, but he was wrong.

A friend of his, Rodney Frank, fed into Essex's growing discontent with the navy by encouraging him to read the works of Black militants. Following an altercation with a white NCO who'd made racist remarks to Essex, he went AWOL from October 19 to February 10, 1970. Essex was discharged for

Mark James Robert Essex, the "New Orleans Sniper," was shot and killed on the roof of the Downtown Howard Johnson's Hotel on January 7, 1973. *Gracen Deerman.*

"general unsuitability" on February 10, 1971. Essex became even more radicalized following his discharge from the navy, immersing himself in Black radical ideology and calling himself "Mata." Two months after returning home to Emporia in April 1971, Essex ordered a Ruger model 55 .44-caliber semiautomatic carbine from Montgomery Ward and began spending hours target shooting.

In August 1971, Essex relocated to Louisiana, moving around to various towns before finally settling down in New Orleans, where he lived alone, gradually sinking into a depression. His growing hatred of white people drove him to purchase a .38-caliber revolver. He finally reached the breaking point on November 16, 1972, when police in Baton Rouge Parish shot and killed two Black demonstrators at Southern University. By December, Essex had given away most of his personal belongings. Shortly before New Year's Eve, Essex sent a letter to WWL-TV declaring his intention to attack the New Orleans Police Department on December 31.

It turned out that Essex was true to his word. On December 31, 1972, he parked his car and walked down Perdido Street to a parking lot across from the New Orleans Police Department. After finding a good hiding place, Essex fired his .44-caliber semiautomatic carbine at two policemen, killing Cadet Alfred Harrell and wounding Lieutenant Horace Perez. Essex quickly climbed a chain-link fence and ran across Highway I-10, confusing his pursuers by tossing lighted firecrackers behind him. When he reached the Gert Town area of New Orleans, he took refuge in the Burkart warehouse, unknowingly setting off a burglar alarm. When the dog unit, consisting of Officers Harold Blappert and Edwin Hosli, arrived on the scene, Essex shot Officer Hosli in the back as he was releasing his German shepherd from the front seat. While he was calling for backup, Officer Blappert fired at the muzzle flashes from Essex's rifle. Blappert managed to pull his wounded partner into the front seat of the police car while waiting for the other officers to arrive. By the time they had reached the warehouse, however, Essex was gone.

Essex struck again on January 7, 1973. At 10:15 a.m., Essex shot a grocer named Joe Perniciaro with his carbine and made his getaway by carjacking Marvin Albert's 1968 Chevrolet Chevelle outside of his house. He drove to the Downtown Howard Johnson's Hotel in New Orleans's business district and began climbing the stairwell. He entered the hotel on the eighteenth floor, the top floor. He was walking down the hallway when he encountered two hotel guests, Dr. Robert Steagall and his wife, Betty, who were on their honeymoon. After shooting Dr. Steagall in the chest and his wife in the back of the head, Essex ran inside their bedroom, room 1829, and set fire to a telephone book and the curtains with lighter fluid. Before exiting the eighteenth floor, Essex dropped a Pan-American flag on the floor next to the Steagalls. He then ran down to the eleventh floor, where he set fire to more rooms, killing the hotel's assistant manager, Frank Schneider, and wounding the hotel's general manager, Walter Collins, in the process. Collins died a few weeks later.

Essex hustled back up to the eighteenth floor, where he shot two policemen who were trying to enter the hotel on a fire truck's ladder. Just a few minutes later, Essex shot two more officers, Phillip Coleman and Paul Persigo, who was shot in the mouth while trying to lead onlookers to safety. From his perch on the eighteenth floor, Essex shot Deputy Superintendent Louis Sirgo in the chest as he was trying to rescue a couple of wounded officers on the staircase. Sirgo was later pronounced dead at Charity Hospital.

With his supply of ammunition and firecrackers depleted, Essex ran up to the roof of the building, where he got into a shoot-out with a helicopter that was firing down at him. Essex retreated to a concrete cubicle on the roof. At 9:00 p.m., Essex emerged from the cubicle and ran out into the open, shouting, "Come and get me!" Almost instantly, his body was riddled with a barrage of bullets from several snipers who were on the roofs of adjacent buildings and the sharpshooter aboard the helicopter. The autopsy revealed that Essex had been shot more than two hundred times. Once the smoke had cleared, officers found that Essex had only two bullets left in his rifle.

Essex left behind twenty-one shooting victims, nine of whom died. Five of the ten officers who were shot died. With the exception of Officer Alfred Harrell, who was Black, all of his victims were white or Hispanic. During Essex's funeral at St. James Church in Emporia, Kansas, two wreaths were placed on his coffin. One of them bore a ribbon with his name printed on it. On the other wreath was the slogan "Power to the People."

DERRICK TODD LEE

THE BATON ROUGE SERIAL KILLER

Born on November 5, 1968, in St. Francisville, Louisiana, Derek Todd Lee most likely developed his antisocial tendencies from growing up in a dysfunctional family. He and his siblings were abandoned by their biological father, who suffered from bipolar disorder. When Derek was three years old, he endured frequent beatings from his stepfather. His mother did nothing to stop the abuse. Lee's situation did not improve very much in school, where his classmates mocked him because he was enrolled in special education classes. Before long, Lee found an outlet for his anger by abusing small animals and peering into the windows of houses in the neighborhood. In his teenage years, Lee's behavior problems came to the attention of the police. However, on several occasions, when he was charged with burglary or voyeurism, he was able to use his powers of persuasion to get himself out of trouble.

By the time Lee was in the eleventh grade, his behavior problems had escalated, forcing him to drop out of school. After a few brushes with the law, including after he burned up his car to collect the insurance, Lee tried to live like a responsible adult. In September 1988, he married Jacqueline Denise Sims, and he fathered two children with her. But the marriage ended in 1989. Afterward, Lee took out his anger on other people. Eventually, he was arrested for starting a fight in a St. Francisville bar. The courts ordered him to seek psychiatric help, but he ignored his appointments.

No one would have guessed that Lee's violent tendencies would lead him to commit a string of murders in the early 2000s. On September 23,

2002, a forty-one-year-old nurse named Gina Wilson Green was found raped and strangled in her Baton Rouge apartment. Then on May 31, 2002, the body of a twenty-two-year-old graduate student named Charlotte Murray Pace was discovered at a townhouse in Baton Rouge, not far from Louisiana State University. Police detectives concluded that she, too, was sexually assaulted and bludgeoned, although evidence suggested that she put up a struggle. The police also found the track of a Rawlings-brand trainer on the floor. Almost six weeks later, a third murder sent shockwaves through Baton Rouge. On July 14, Pam Kinamore, the owner of an antique shop, disappeared. When her husband arrived home from work, he became alarmed when he saw his wife's car

Derek Todd Lee preyed on women in Baton Rouge before he died in Louisiana State Penitentiary's hospital on January 23, 2016. *Gracen Deerman.*

in the driveway but she was nowhere to be found. On July 16, a survey crew working in a marshy area between Baton Rouge and Lafayette made a gruesome discovery. Lying in the shallow water was the corpse of a naked woman. A knife wound in her neck was clearly visible. Later, investigators reported that she had been sexually molested and that her silver toe ring was missing. They identified the body as being that of Pam Kinamore. Police were aided in their search for the killer by a twenty-eight-year-old Mississippi woman who claimed she had been raped by a man who dragged her into a white pickup truck on Interstate Highway 10 near Baton Rouge. Fortunately, she was able to give police a detailed description of her assailant. Another witness provided investigators with more valuable information. She told them that on July 13, she saw the limp figure of a woman sitting in the passenger seat of a white pickup truck driving down the interstate at 3:00 a.m. She lost sight of the truck when it turned off the highway on the Whisky Bay exit, the same area where Kinamore's body was found.

In August 2002, a task force consisting of members of police departments, sheriff's departments, the FBI and the Louisiana State Police took over the investigation. Using DNA evidence collected from the bodies of Gina Lee and Charlotte Pace, they determined that the same man had killed both of them. Convinced that a serial killer was on the loose in the Baton Rouge area, the investigators began examining the unsolved murders of other women in cold case files. A few months later, another homicide was added to the list. On November 24, 2002, a rabbit hunter found the nude body of a twenty-three-year-old, Trineisha Dene Colomb, who had vanished three days before. An ex-marine, Colomb had tried to fight off her assailant while he was stabbing her to death. This case stood out, not only because it was the first time the serial killer had struck outside of Baton Rouge but also because his victim was Black. Once again, a white pickup truck was sighted in the area. Drawing from the evidence collected at the crime scene, a criminal profiler deduced that the killer was probably a strong man who worked at a physically demanding occupation and who stalked his victims.

Despite the progress made in the case, the murders continued. On March 3, another Louisiana State student, twenty-six-year-old Carrie Lynn Yoder, left the home where she lived alone and drove to Winn-Dixie to do some grocery shopping. Her boyfriend, Lee Stanton, was puzzled when she did not call him back later that evening as she said she would. The next day, when he still had not heard from Carrie, he drove to her home and walked inside. He immediately noticed that a key rack hanging just inside the doorway was hanging by a single screw, indicating that it had been dislodged during a struggle. No trace of Carrie Yoder was found until March 14, when a fisherman discovered her badly beaten corpse floating in the Atchafalaya River, not far from the place where Pam Kinamore's body had also been found. Investigators could tell that Yoder had fought back with all of her might while she was being choked to death.

Just one week later, another woman vanished under mysterious circumstances. Melinda McGhee, a thirty-one-year-old resident of Atmore, Alabama, was working at her job at a nursing home when she called her mother and husband around 8:30 a.m. Police believe that she was abducted when she returned home because of the obvious signs of a struggle that had taken place between McGhee and someone else. Her body was never found. Similarities between her case and those of Kinamore and Yoder led police to believe that they were all victims of the same murderer.

The task force added another name to the list of potential victims in April. The body of a fifty-two-year-old sex worker named Lillian Robins was found in the Atchafalaya River near the Whiskey Bay Bridge. Friends and relatives had reported her missing the month before.

The Baton Rouge serial killer may have claimed another victim in May 2002, when a twenty-three-year-old Louisiana State student named Christine

Moore disappeared after driving to a park in Baton Rouge where she jogged occasionally. Foul play was suspected when her car was found abandoned not far from River Road. When her body was found, it was clear that the young woman had been stabbed to death. Despite the similarities between her murder and those of the other women, she was not formally listed as one of the victims of the Baton Rouge serial killer.

Initially, the FBI profiled the murderer as a white male between the ages of twenty-five and thirty-five. Later, though, a Florida lab that examined the evidence found that the killer was probably a Black male. On May 5, 2003, authorities compared DNA taken from Derrick Todd Lee three weeks earlier with evidence collected from the crime scenes. After matching Lee's DNA with the forensic evidence, FBI agents concluded that Lee had murdered Green, Pace, Kinamore, Colomb and Yoder. By this time, Lee had fled Louisiana, but investigators tracked him to Atlanta. They apprehended Lee on May 27, 2003. He was formally indicted on September 24, 2003. The next week, a nurse named Diane Alexander accused Lee of attempting to rape her after beating her. Lee was also charged with the second-degree murder of twenty-one-year-old Geralyn De Soto. The jury found him guilty of the murders of Geralyn DeSoto and Charlotte Murray Pace. Although Lee was sentenced to die, he cheated the executioner by passing away from heart disease at Louisiana State Penitentiary's hospital on January 21, 2016.

ANNE PLUE GATES

THE LOUISIANA BLACK WIDOW

Sexual cannibalism is considered by most people to be a characteristic of the lower forms of life. The females of several species of snakes, mantises and spiders have been known to kill and eat their mates during and after copulation. As human beings, we view ourselves as being far above such "cold-blooded behavior," which is the reason why women who kill their husbands or lovers are called "black widows." A prime example from Louisiana is Anne Plue Gates.

Anne Gibson was born in 1949 in Indiana. While growing up in Lewisville, Indiana, she was shamelessly spoiled by her parents, probably because she was an only child. A childhood friend of hers named Tim Conwell said that when Anne was a child, she "got away with a lot of stuff."

After graduating from high school, Anne enrolled in nursing school and worked as a nurse. In 1977, she married a Vietnam War veteran named David Plue, who was working at a Chrysler automobile factory at the time. Their marriage proved to be short-lived. Anne's murderous side first surfaced on May 28, 1978, when the body of her husband was found along a rural highway. He had been killed execution style with two bullets to the head. Initially, Anne was not a prime suspect, probably because the lies that she told investigators had the ring of truth. Their suspicions became aroused, however, when they discovered that Plue had a $100,000 insurance policy from his place of work and that after his death, Anne used the money to buy a home in Picayune, Mississippi, so that she could live near her parents. However, the investigation of Anne's role in her husband's death came to a dead end when it became apparent that most of the evidence that had been collected was circumstantial.

Not long after moving to Picayune, Anne met Raymond Gates. Born in Omaha, Nebraska, in 1922, Gates was stationed in New Orleans during World War II. He liked the area so much that he decided to move back there after the war. After earning his accounting degree, Gates got a job at Tidewater Inc., a small shipping company. Despite the fact that Gates was twenty-six years older than Anne, she was attracted to his genteel demeanor and married him in December 1978. She was his second wife. Gates's first wife had died from an aneurysm in 1971. In the early 1980s, the couple built a house in Arabi, Louisiana, in St. Bernard Parish.

Anne Plue Gates, the Louisiana "Black Widow," married the man she had blamed for the death of her second husband. *Gracen Deerman.*

On October 3, 1987, police received a frantic phone call from Anne Gates, who claimed that when she returned home from picking up the mail, she found her husband's inert body lying on the floor. When the police arrived on the scene and examined the corpse, they found that the man had been beaten repeatedly in the head by something like a fireplace poker. Most of the crime scene was soaked in blood; there was no sign of forced entry. Later, the coroner determined that Raymond Gates had been dead for several days. At the time, the retired nurse was living with her mother in Picayune, Mississippi. She explained to investigators that she had not seen her husband since September 30. She went on to say that she and her husband had sort of an open marriage. She lived with Raymond for a couple of days each week; with her boyfriend in Metairie, Louisiana, for a couple days each week; and with her parents the rest of the week. She added that her husband "saw other people" during her absences.

Investigators became convinced of Anne's involvement in her husband's death after examining the contents of his will. If Raymond died first, Anne stood to inherit his entire estate. If she died first, then the estate would go to her mother, Ileane Gibson. Anne was also named the beneficiary of his $82,000 insurance policy. In 1987, Anne was arrested and charged with second-degree murder. Two years later, she pleaded no contest to manslaughter charges in her husband's death. In Louisiana, a person convicted of murder can be removed from the murder victim's will. However, Anne's lawyers argued that this stipulation did not apply to their client because she did not admit guilt when she pleaded no contest. In 1992, a settlement granted Anne and her mother $25,000 each from her husband's life insurance and the sale of the house. Gates's relatives divided the rest among themselves.

As part of her plea deal, Anne blamed her friend Tim Conwell for Raymond Gates's death. Because of the lack of physical evidence, Conwell was released.

RONALD JOSEPH DOMINIQUE

THE BAYOU SERIAL KILLER

Born on January 9, 1964, Ronald Joseph Dominique grew up in Thibodaux, a small Louisiana town sandwiched between Baton Rouge and New Orleans. In high school, Dominique gained a reputation for being a homosexual, possibly because of his participation in the glee club and the chorus, but he denied the accusations. After high school, however, Dominique began to act on his homosexual inclinations, although he did so surreptitiously. To his neighbors, he was a kind, civic-minded young man who was attentive to the needs of his neighbors in the trailer parks where he lived. At night and on weekends, however, he turned himself into Patti LaBelle at the nearby gay bar, giving what many recall as a very bad impression of the singer.

As an adult, Dominique never really had a home of his own, choosing to live with his sister, mother and other relatives. In his twenties, he was charged with a series of minor offenses, such as disturbing the peace, battery and traffic violations. On June 12, 1984, Dominique was charged with telephone harassment. On May 15, 1994, he was charged with speeding while intoxicated. He was charged with his first sexual crime on August 25, 1996, when a half-naked young man jumped out of the window of Dominique's room, claiming that Dominique had tried to kill him. On February 10, 2002, Dominique was arrested for slapping a woman in a parking lot in Terribonne Parish during a Mardi Gras parade after she hit a baby stroller with her car. He was never tried for the offense because he chose to enter a parish offenders program instead. On May 19, 2000, Dominique paid a fine for disturbing the peace. Dominique was never charged with rape because the victim refused to testify. The judge chose to continue the case instead of dismissing it altogether.

Unknown to Dominique's friends, relatives and neighbors, this rather nondescript, harmless-looking "loser" was actually a vicious serial killer who preyed on runaways, homeless people and homosexuals between 1997 and 2005. He escaped detection for as long as he did by choosing people who were leading what were considered "marginal" lifestyles. His modus operandi rarely varied from one encounter to the next. After meeting his potential victims, ranging in age from sixteen to forty-six, in the street, a bar or a club, he asked them to accompany him to his camper-trailer for sex. If the man was heterosexual, Dominique promised the man that he could have sex with his (nonexistent) wife, who preferred that her partners be tied up. After Dominique had bound his victims, he raped them, strangled them or smothered them. Once his victims were dead, he placed them in the trunk of his vehicle and transported them to dumping sites in one of six jurisdictions in southern Louisiana.

Dominique's killing spree ended in 2006 when an ex-con told police that a man had approached him about having a ménage à trois with him and his wife. However, when the ex-con went to the man's trailer, he got "spooked" and took off. Investigators followed up on the man's description of the trailer and located it in Blue Bayou. They then traced the trailer back to Dominique, who had previously been living in a homeless shelter in Homa. During his interrogation, Dominique agreed to submit samples of his DNA, which connected him to the murders of two men in Jefferson Parish in 1998 and 1999. A task force had been formed in 1997 to investigate a series of unsolved murders in Terrebonne, Lafourche and Iberville Parishes and in suburban New Orleans, and discovered the half-dressed corpses of a number of men who had been strangled or smothered, for the most part. On December 1, 2006, Dominique was arrested for the murders of two men, nineteen-year-old Manuel Reed and twenty-seven-year-old Oliver Lebanks.

After Dominique was arrested and confessed to twenty-three murders, however, he blamed the deaths of his victims on their addictions. He also argued that his victims voluntarily agreed to being tied up and/or handcuffed because they wanted to be paid. Dominique claimed he released any potential victim who refused to be tied up. During his trial, prosecutors offered him a plea bargain, and he accepted it. On September 24, 2008, the jury found Dominique guilty on all charges. He was sentenced to life in prison without parole.

In the interviews that were collected, many of Dominique's acquaintances expressed surprise that he was a serial killer. Most of them characterized him as being "weird" but definitely not a murderer. The owner of the gay club where he trolled for many of his victims recalled that Dominique was not very well liked. One patron of the club went so far as to say that his inability to "fit in" with the gay community could account for the anger that drove him to murder the people who had rejected him.

ANTOINETTE FRANK

GOOD COP GONE WRONG

In the early 1990s, the image of the New Orleans Police Department was tarnished by the criminal activities of more than forty officers, which included bank robbery, rape, aggravated battery and narcotics charges. In 1995, the most sensationalistic arrest of several police officers in connection with murder was that of former police officer Antoinette Frank.

According to psychologists, Frank's erratic behavior as an adult can be traced back to her troubled childhood. Her father spent little time with his family, a fact that might account for her brother's several brushes with the law while Frank was growing up. Because she had always wanted to be a policewoman, Frank neglected to mention her psychological issues when she applied for a job as a law enforcement officer in New Orleans. Not long after she joined the police force, Frank and her partner, Ronald Williams, were hired as part-time security guards for Kim Anh, a Vietnamese restaurant in New Orleans East. The owners of the restaurant, the Vu family, were very fond of Frank, even going so far as to loan her money and give her birthday presents. Frank's sweet demeanor began to erode after she began bringing her boyfriend, Roger LaCaze, to the restaurant for lunch. She had become romantically involved with LaCaze, a reputed drug dealer, when she came to his aid after he was wounded during a shooting. Before long, rumors began spreading that she was so enamored of the eighteen-year-old that she let him drive her police car around. When the Vus started paying Ronald Williams more money than Frank, she and LaCaze began plotting ways to make up for the discrepancy in their wages.

On March 4, 1995, Frank had just finished her meal when she slipped into the back and stole the keys to the restaurant. After midnight, Frank and LaCaze returned to Kim Anh in Frank's police car. While Chau Vu was counting the day's earnings, she noticed the pair walking stealthily to the front door. Suspecting that Frank and LaCaze were up to no good, Chau hastily hid the money in the microwave. Using the key she had stolen, Frank walked into the restaurant and pushed two employees into the kitchen doorway. When Williams walked into the doorway to find out what was going on, LaCaze snuck up behind Frank's partner and fired several shots into his neck, head

Policewoman Antoinette Frank teamed up with a drug dealer named Roger LaCaze to rob a Vietnamese restaurant. *Gracen Deerman.*

and back. As soon as Frank turned toward the restaurant dining room, Chau grabbed the arm of another employee, Quoc, and ran into the cooler. While hiding in the cooler, Chau heard Frank yelling at her sister and brother, Ha and Cuong, who were busy sweeping the dining room floor. Frank demanded that they tell her the location of the money. Frustrated, Frank pistol-whipped Cuong when he claimed that he did not know where the money was hidden. To avoid being struck again, Cuong told her that the money was stashed in the microwave. After he handed it to her, she shot Ha three times as she begged for mercy. Frank also shot Cuong six times.

Frank and LaCaze then fled the premises with their stolen loot. Frank decided that the best way to cover her tracks was for her to drop LaCaze off at an apartment complex and return to the scene of the crime. Frank borrowed a police car and drove back to the restaurant, posing as one of the responding officers. When Chau bolted through the front door, Frank informed her that she was one of the arresting officers. Chau recognized Frank as one of the two robbers and told the other officers that Frank was one of the shooters. After the officers interrogated Chau and Frank at different tables in the restaurant, Frank was transported to the police station for questioning, where she admitted that she and LaCaze had committed the crimes.

A New Orleans Parish grand jury indicted Frank and LaCaze on April 28, 1995. LaCaze's trial lasted from July 17 to July 21, 1995. At the conclusion of LaCaze's trial, the jury found him guilty and sentenced him to death. Frank's trial began on September 5, 1995, and ended on September 12, 1995, with a guilty verdict on all counts and a life sentence, probably because the evidence against her was so strong that her attorney did not mount a very strong defense. She was sent to death row at Louisiana Correctional Institute. Several years after the conviction, Frank claimed that she had been beaten, sexually abused and impregnated by her father. In November 1995, two years after Frank reported her father missing, a dog led investigators to a human skull buried under Frank's house. The skull had a bullet hole in it. At the time of this writing, the case is still open.

RUSSELL ELLWOOD

NEW ORLEANS'S KILLER TAXI DRIVER

Some of history's most vicious murderers are actually rather nondescript individuals whom few people would even notice on the street. One of Louisiana's most ruthless killers, Russell Ellwood, is described in *Murderpedia* as a "serial loser" about whom very little is known prior to his murderous rampage in the 1990s. Evidence indicates that he might have been born in Massillon, Ohio. Following his high school graduation in 1968, Ellwood moved to New Orleans, where he worked at a variety of dead-end jobs, mostly as a freelance photographer and taxi driver. Because of his addiction to street drugs, Ellwood's living conditions were squalid at best. When he was particularly short on funds, he even slept in his taxicab. Ellwood's financial difficulties were exacerbated by his fondness for get-rich-quick schemes, none of which panned out for him. The only true windfall in his life was his $15,000 inheritance from his mother, which he squandered on penny stocks.

In the early 1990s, Ellwood embarked on a killing spree that lasted until 1997. Most of his victims were Black drug-addicted prostitutes, whose corpses were discovered in swampy areas. His first known victim, Cheryl Lewis, was drowned between February 1 and February 3, 1993, and thrown into a canal. Ellwood is believed to have taken her body to Hahnville, Louisiana, some time later and dumped it alongside Highway 3160. The girl's mother filed a missing persons report with the police the next day. Ellwood's next victim was Lillian Dolores Mack. Ellwood drugged her

New Orleans taxi driver Russell Ellwood is suspected of murdering over fifteen women. *Gracen Deerman.*

first and then killed her. Lewis's body was discovered on February 21, and Mack's body was found on February 22. Supporting the belief held by many criminologists that murderers feel compelled to return to the scene of the crime, Ellwood showed up in the middle of the night at the place where he had drowned Lewis. Coincidentally, two off-duty St. Charles police deputies spotted his taxi parked along the road. He told them that he pulled off the road so that he could change his oil and dump the old oil someplace where no one could see him. The deputies thought it was odd that they could not find any evidence that Ellwood had changed the oil, but they let him go anyway.

This strange encounter with Ellwood led a task force to name him as a suspect in 1997. During an interview in Sebring, Florida, Ellwood told investigators that he had dreamed the task force would be interested in interviewing him. Their suspicions that Ellwood might be a serial killer were confirmed on August 4, 1997, after he was arrested for buying drugs from an undercover police officer and sentenced to serve eighty-five days in jail in Florida. While Ellwood was incarcerated, he told some of the other inmates about the women he had killed. Following his release, Ellwood was placed on probation. Ellwood decided to travel to Canton, Ohio, so he could work for his brother. During this time, Ellwood was interviewed once again by the serial killer task force. This time, he admitted that he drove down a country road and dumped the corpse of a Black female in the water. As a result of his confession, Ellwood was charged with two counts of second-degree murder. During his trial, the testimony of several inmates led to his conviction on one count of murder, but the second count of murder was dropped on February 2, 1999, when it came out in court that Ellwood was in Ohio at the time of the murder. Eventually, he confessed to killing Lewis and Mack, but because he refused to be recorded, Ellwood denied making the confession sometime later and was released.

Ellwood returned to New Orleans, where he was cited by the police for speeding. Because Ellwood did not appear on the appointed court date, he was charged with contempt of court and incarcerated for 120 days. Before he was released, he was charged with the murders of Lewis and Mack on March 4, 1998. Ellwood was tried in Lafayette, Louisiana, on June 8, 1999. Several of Ellwood's acquaintances from jail testified that he had boasted about killing two Black sex workers. Then two former prostitutes testified that he had beaten and raped them. Three more witnesses claimed they had seen Ellwood with Lewis around the time of her disappearance. When Ellwood took the stand, he denied knowing Lewis or Mack, but he provided no evidence to support his claim. Despite the fact that Lewis's mother stated she had never seen Ellwood in her daughter's presence, he was found guilty of murdering Lewis and sentenced to life in prison. The court decided not to charge Ellwood with Mack's murder.

At the time of Ellwood's arrest in 1997, he was suspected of murdering at least fifteen other women, but no charges were filed against him. Authorities believe that he plied most of his victims with drugs before strangling or suffocating them. All of these murders remain unsolved. Ellwood's motive for killing these women was never determined. He died in Angola State Prison in 2014.

SEAN VINCENT GILLIS

THE SCOURGE OF BATON ROUGE

Sean Vincent Gillis was born on June 24, 1962. While he was growing up, his family life was far from ideal. His father, Norman Gillis, suffered from alcoholism and mental illness. His frequent stays in mental institutions played an important role in his son's life. Nevertheless, Yvonne, who worked at a local television station, managed to make a happy home for her son. When Gillis was ten years old, he and his mother moved to another neighborhood, where his behavior problems first began to surface. Over the next few weeks, he earned a reputation as a bully. Convinced that her son needed a more structured learning environment, Yvonne sent him to a Catholic elementary school. When Gillis was in the seventh grade, he attended Redemptorist High School. In 1980, he and a friend became involved in activities that got the attention of the police, such as driving while intoxicated, smoking marijuana and participating in satanic rituals. That same year, Gillis's relationship with his father began to show signs of improvement. However, their close bond deteriorated rapidly when Norman discovered his son's photographs of naked men in various sexual positions.

Following his graduation from high school, Gillis started working at a 7-11 convenience store. When his boss began moving him from one 7-11 store to the next, Gillis's interest in being a good employee waned. He spent most of his time at work surfing porn sites. After a while, he became so adept at using computers that he decided to apply for admission to the local community college to become certified in computer technology. When Yvonne found a new job in Atlanta and asked him to move there with her, he refused. Even though his mother tried to stay in contact with her son by paying his mortgage, he found it increasingly difficult to cope with her absence. Neighbors said he occasionally stepped outside and screamed curse words to no one in particular. Gillis also began having brushes with the law. When a woman complained that Gillis was peeking in her window, he told the police that he was looking for his cat. Gillis was also stopped by the police for traffic violations. In 1994, Gillis tried build other relationships in his life. He went out on a date with a woman named Terri Lemoine. After a while, they began arguing, and Terri slapped him, causing him to burst into tears. She promised never to do it again.

Gillis's emotionally fragile state deteriorated not long thereafter. On March 21, 1994, Gillis entered an exclusive retirement home named St. James Place, across the street from where he worked, and attacked an eighty-two-year-old artist and musician named Ann Bryan. She had left the front door of her apartment ajar so that her nurse could enter. Gillis initially intended to rape her, but he lost control when she started screaming and stabbed her forty-seven times, disemboweling her and slashing her throat so deeply that he severed her head. Later, he claimed that he killed her because of "stress."

By 1995, Gillis was living with Teri Lemoine, who turned a blind eye to his obsession with pornography and the photographs he showed her of dead women. On January 5, 1999, Gillis gave in to his bloodlust and murdered a second woman. He invited a twenty-nine-year-old sex worker named Katherine Hall into his car on the pretext of wanting oral sex. Once she was in the car, Gillis attempted, unsuccessfully, to strangle her with a nylon twist tie. While she tried to escape, he stabbed her sixteen times. Not only did he cut her legs and stab her in her torso, but he also cut off her eyelids. When he was sure she was dead, he undressed her and stabbed her twenty-one more times. As the investigators were examining the crime scene, they found a hair that they later determined belonged to a white male.

In May 1999, Gillis focused his attention on an avid jogger, fifty-two-year-old Hardee Schmidt, whom he saw running in South Baton Rouge. For the next three weeks, he drove around Baton Rouge, looking for her. Finally, on May 30, 1999, he spotted Schmidt running through Pollard Estates on her morning run. He struck her with his car and knocked her into a ditch, where her body would not be visible to passing vehicles. Gillis then tied a zip tie around her neck and forced her to climb into his trunk. He drove to BREC Park, where he raped his victim. After killing her, he placed her naked body back in the trunk of his white Chevy Cavalier. Schmidt's corpse remained

Sean Vincent Gillis, Baton Rouge's "pure evil" serial killer, raped and murdered a female jogger in BREC Forest Community Park. *Wikimedia Commons.*

in Gillis's car for two days. Finally, he drove the woman's corpse to a bayou off Highway 61 in St. James Parish and dumped it there. The body was discovered just a few days later.

Gillis resumed his crime spree almost six months later on November 12, 1999. He was driving on Highway 19 in Scotlandville when he spotted Joyce Williams walking along the roadside. Williams was well known in her community for her singing and dancing. Gillis picked her up and drove her around for a while, singing songs on the radio, before stopping at a lonely spot on Rosedale Road in Port Allen. After strangling the woman with a nylon zip tie, Gillis drove home. He carried her corpse into his house and then proceeded to cut it into pieces, some of which he consumed. After he was full, Gillis placed the remaining body parts in a Xerox box and garbage bags and dumped them in Iberville Parish.

Gillis gave a ride to his next victim as well. Fifty-two-year-old Lillian Robinson was in North Baton Rouge when Gillis picked her up in January 2000. Somewhere on the way to his house, Gillis strangled her with a nylon zip tie. After he took her body to his house, Gillis mutilated it and then drove to Atchafalaya Basin, where he dumped it in a swampy area. She was listed as a "missing person" until her body was found nine miles from the dump site.

Gillis's next victim almost got away from him. In October 2000, he was on his way to visit his godchild when he saw that thirty-eight-year-old Marilyn Nevils was in need of a ride. As soon as Marilyn sat down in his car, Gillis reached for a nylon zip tie, but she was able to fight him off and run into a field on Sixth Street. Gillis was finally able to subdue Marilyn by striking her on the head with a large piece of rebar. To make sure she was dead, Gillis tied a nylon zip tie around her neck. Before taking her body to his house, Gillis removed it from his car while he washed it out. Before driving her body to another dumping site, Gillis cleaned himself and his victim in the shower at his house. After he finished, Gillis drove along the River Road to a levee, where he laid her body down. At the time, no one had reported her as missing.

Not all of Gillis's victims were complete strangers. Forty-five-year-old Johnnie Mae Williams not only smoked marijuana with Gillis, but she also periodically worked as his cleaning lady. On October 9, 2003, their relationship came to a bloody end. Gillis drove her from North Baton Rouge to an out-of-the-way spot behind Mason's Grill, where he bludgeoned her to death and cut her numerous times on her back and legs. To make the identification of her body difficult, Gillis removed her hands before dumping the rest of her body in the woods in Zachary. However, after her body was discovered, a family friend was able to identify her remains anyway. Before leaving the scene, Gillis photographed her body. She was the mother of three children.

Gillis's reign of terror ended in February 2004 when he picked up his last victim, forty-three-year-old Donna Bennet Johnson, in North Baton Rouge and drove her to an isolated location near Scenic Highway. Once again, his modus operandi did not go as planned. Just as Gillis was trying to wrap the nylon zip tie around her neck, she managed to wrest herself out of his grasp and leap out of the car. She had just made it to a nearby fence when Gillis caught up with her and killed her. He put Johnston's body in the trunk of his car, took forty-five pictures of it and then drove it to Parkway Drive, where he dismembered it. He also ate parts of her body before finally hiding it in a drainage canal near Ben Hur Road in Baton Rouge.

Meanwhile, a task force made up of state and local police was created to search for a connection between Johnston's murder and the murders of two other victims of Gillis. During an investigation of Johnston's dump site in April 2004, investigators reported that they had found an arm that had been severed at the elbow. They also discovered that that the torso's nipples had been cut off and that a crude attempt had made to cut out a tattoo on her right thigh. Their most important discovery was tire tracks found at the scene, which police were able to trace to a model of tire that was manufactured between 2001 and 2003. On April 28, the officers then interviewed local people who owned this type of tire. They also took DNA samples from them and tried to match them with the DNA found on the bodies of two of Gillis's victims. When Gillis's DNA was found to be a match with the DNA that was found on the victims' bodies, he was taken into custody the next day. He apologized to Teri, who was present at the time of his arrest. Gillis confessed to the murders a few hours later. He told the police that he must have been "pure evil" to commit a series of murders as brutal as these were.

An investigation of Gillis's house produced even more incriminating evidence. Investigators found forty-five digital pictures of Johnston's butchered corpse, as well as photographs of her corpse lying in the trunk of his car. They also discovered that Gillis had taken some of the body parts of his victims to his home as souvenirs.

On July 21, 2008, Gillis was tried for the murders of Katherine Hall, Johnnie Mae Williams and Donna Bennett Johnston. Although he was found guilty on all counts, the jury was deadlocked in the penalty phase of the trial. Gillis was eventually sentenced to life in prison on July 31. On February 17, 2009, he was given another life sentence after pleading guilty to the murder of Joyce Williams.

NATHANIEL ROBERT CODE JR.

THE SHREVEPORT SERIAL KILLER

Most of the people who knew Nathaniel Robert Code Jr. while he was growing up in the Bel-Air neighborhood of Shreveport, Louisiana, were probably not surprised to find out that he became a serial killer. In his early teens, he had a reputation of being a bully and a sadist who once doused an animal in lighter fluid and set it on fire. Local authorities connected him with the death of a gay man nicknamed "Granny," who was said to have purchased alcohol for minors in exchange for sex. The police believed that Code beat the man to death with an iron skillet because other teens called him "Granny Jr.," but they did not have enough evidence to charge him with the crime. Even Code's stepmother and best friend admitted that he was a "decent" but troubled child. After Code dropped out of high school, his life took a downward spiral. In 1975, when he was nineteen years old, Code sneaked into a woman's home through a window and tried to rape her. Around the same time, two doctors diagnosed Code with paranoid schizophrenia. He was sentenced to serve a fifteen-year sentence for the attempted rape charge, but he was released after only five years. Following his release from prison, Code worked a series of low-paying jobs, such as mowing lawns or house-sitting, to pay for his growing cocaine habit.

In August 1984, only eight months after being released from prison, Code committed his first in a series of murders in Shreveport's Cedar Grove neighborhood that ended in 1987. On August 30, 1984, a Black twenty-five-year-old single mother named Deborah Ford returned from a shopping trip with her two daughters to her house on East Seventy-Fourth Street. After a friend took the girls to their grandmother's house, Deborah fell asleep on the couch. Unknown to Deborah, her house was being watched by a man with murder in his heart, Nathaniel Robert Code Jr. Shortly after midnight, he entered the house through a bathroom window. She tried to resist him, but he punched her several times until she fell unconscious and tied her up with an electrical cord from her box fan before stabbing her nineteen times. Then, in what amounted to "overkill," he cut her throat so deeply that she was almost decapitated. After her bloody corpse was discovered at 8:00 a.m. the next morning by her friend Brenda Greggs, Code, who lived just a few houses down, joined the crowd that gathered around the yellow police tape at the crime scene. The crime was so brutal that the coroner, George McCormick, predicted Ford's murderer would kill again. McCormick also pointed out the killer's signature elements, such as the binding of Ford with an electrical cord and the use of a unique ligature that would probably turn up again in later murders.

On July 19, 1985, Code attacked another house in his neighborhood. This time, it was a house at 213 East Seventy-Second Street, where Vivian Chaney lived with her boyfriend, Billy Joe Harris. Chaney's brother, Jerry Culbert, and her three daughters, Carlitha Culbert, Tomika Chaney and Marla Chaney, also lived in the house. Tomika and Marla were mentally disabled. Code forced open the back door of the Chaney house between 11:39 p.m. on July 18, 1985, and 6:00 a.m. on July 19, 1985. Billy Joe Harris, who was twenty-nine years old, was lying in the front bedroom bed when the police arrived on the scene. Code had tied Harris's hands behind his back with shoelaces using a handcuff ligature. Code shot him twice in the left side of his head through a pillow to muffle the sound. He shot Harris twice in the chest as well, but miraculously, he was still alive, so Code slit his throat. Code tied Harris's hands to his ankles using a telephone cord. Harris was probably asleep when he was assaulted.

Vivian Chaney's brother, Jerry Culbert (twenty-five), was also probably asleep when Code killed him in the back bedroom. He was shot in the left side of the head. However, Code did not bind him with ligatures.

In the living room, the authorities found fifteen-year-old Carlitha Culbert lying on her stomach. Her hands were tied behind her with an electrical cord, once again in a handcuff ligature. Code had tried to gag her with duct tape. He'd also slashed her throat so deeply that he almost decapitated her.

Vivian Chaney (thirty-seven) was inside the bathtub, leaning over the side, when the police found her. Like Harris and Carlitha's, Vivian's hands were tied behind her back with an electrical cord. It appeared Code had strangled her with his hands and with ligatures.

On July 19, 1985, at 6:00 a.m., Vivian and Jerry's sister, Shirley Culbert, showed up at their front door. She had not told them she was coming. When she heard the radio playing, she walked around the house to the back door. The door was unlocked, so she walked inside. As she was walking toward the girls' bedroom, she noticed that several items were missing. As soon as the girls were awake, they began crying. Sensing that something terrible had happened, she rushed the girls outside the house and called the police.

On August 5, 1986, Nathaniel Code's grandfather William Code was working in the yard of his Shreveport home with the two grandsons of his friend Enamerteen William. At 8:00 p.m., the mother of the two boys, eight-year-old Eric Williams and twelve-year-old Joe Robinson, gave them permission to spend the night at William Code's house, just as they had done before. By noon the next day, she became worried, so she walked over to William Code's house. She knocked on the front door, but no one answered. Oddly enough, the television was on. She peered through the window and caught her breath in surprise when she saw Joe Robinson's bound foot. Mrs. Williams rushed home and called the police. While waiting for them to arrive, she and her brother, niece and granddaughter returned to William Code's house and entered it with a key one of them had brought along. They were shocked to find the bodies of William Code, Eric Williams and Joe Robinson in separate rooms.

All of the bodies bore the trademarks of the Shreveport serial killer. Lying on his bed was the body of William Code, who had obviously been hit very hard on the side of the head, probably with someone's fist. He had also been stabbed five times in the back and once in the right upper arm, most likely with some kind of long knife. Eric's body was lying face down between two small beds. A handcuff ligature had been used to tie his hands, and a white plastic cord had been used to tie his ankles. He had been strangled with another electrical cord. Joe Robinson was found lying on the living room couch. He, too, had been struck in the head. A plastic cord had been used to tie his hands and ankles. He had been strangled with a double length of cord. Of the three victims, William Code was beaten the most severely.

While the investigators were at the crime scene, Nathaniel Code was in his own home with his cousin Beatrice Holmes. After sharing a gram of cocaine, the pair drove to the liquor store and bought some beer. Before returning home, they also bought another gram of cocaine. They were snorting the cocaine when Code received a phone call giving him the bad news regarding his grandfather's death.

After talking on the phone, Code went over to the crime scene and began talking to the police. He told them that the night before the murders, his grandfather had asked him to come to his house because a crowd of people outside were making him nervous. Riding his bicycle, Code arrived at his grandfather's house at 2:00 a.m. on August 5. He told the officers that he did a walk-through of the house and checked the front and backyards as well but found nothing out of the ordinary. From the perspective of the investigating officers, the most interesting part of his testimony was the part in which he mentioned touching the fan, humidifier and vacuum while he was at the house, because the electrical cords used to bind the bodies were taken from these items.

Nathaniel Code was charged with the first-degree murders of Vivian Culbert Chaney, Carlitha Culbert, Jerry Culbert and Billy Joe Harris. His twenty-three-day trial began on September 17, 1990. In order to give the jurors a sense of the brutality of the murders, the prosecution displayed graphic photographs and video footage of the murder victims' bodies. The most convincing evidence presented by the prosecuting attorneys included Code's handprint on the bathtub where Vivian Chaney was drowned and the testimony of an eyewitness, Oscar Washington, who was jogging the night of the murders and saw Code covered in blood. Additional evidence collected at Code's house included duct tape and several pieces of electrical cord. Testimony given in the trial revealed that Code had tried to get loans from several individuals just prior to the murders. He even offered to serve as a paid confidential informant for the Shreveport narcotics officers because

At the time of this writing, serial killer Nathaniel Robert Code Jr. is on death row in Louisiana State Penitentiary. *Wikimedia Commons.*

he needed $100 to pay off a drug dealer. The coroner for Caddo Parish, Dr. McCormick, testified that all of the Shreveport serial killer murders had been committed by the same person because they all bore similarities in the ways the victims were killed. The signature aspect of the crimes was the handcuff binding with an electrical cord.

The jury took its first vote on October 6, 1990. Because eleven of the twelve jurors voted to convict Code of first-degree murder, the jurors took a second vote. Despite the fact that most of the evidence against Code was circumstantial, the jury returned a verdict of guilty of murder in the first degree after deliberating for an hour and twelve additional minutes. Code's defense attorney's emotional plea to the jury to spare his client from the death penalty had no effect. At the time of this writing, Nathaniel Code Jr. is still on death row.

ZACK BOWEN

THE KATRINA CANNIBAL

orn in Bakersfield, California, on May 15, 1978, Zachary "Zack" Bowen spent his formative years in the Golden State. To all appearances, he was the "all-American boy." As he entered his preteens, Zack became overly concerned with other people's opinions of him. By the time he was in high school, Zack was suffering from bouts of depression. Hoping that a change of scenery would improve his mood, Zack left his mother's home behind in California and moved to New Orleans, Louisiana, to live with his father. After graduation, Zack was hired as a bartender. Within a few months, eighteen-year-old Zack became involved in a romantic relationship with a twenty-eight-year-old stripper named Lana Shupack. A few months later, when Lana became pregnant, the couple decided to get married. After the birth of their first child, Zack decided that he would make more money—and become a better provider for his wife and child—if he quit his job as bartender and enlisted in the military. Zack was soon assigned to Kosovo and Iraq, where he served as a military officer. Soon, he was promoted to first sergeant. However, because of his constant exposure to the suffering of the civilian population, especially the death of an Iraqi boy he had befriended in a mortar attack, Zack eventually developed PTSD. When his deteriorating mental state began affecting his behavior, Zack was granted a general discharge, which differed from an honorable discharge in that he was unable to receive educational benefits, a fact that bothered him.

When Zack returned home, the trauma he had endured in Iraq placed a severe strain on his marriage. After a few months, he and Lana separated.

Zack returned to the only other job he ever knew—bartending—to pay child support for his two children. Before long, Zack became close to one of his coworkers, a transplant from the Northeast named Addie Hall. According to her friends, Addie was a "free spirit" who enjoyed expressing her creative side through art, poetry, dancing and sewing. Like Zack, though, Addie was plagued by her personal demons. They found that they both enjoyed "living on the wild side," spending much of their time after work partying.

In 2005, the lives of the residents of New Orleans were altered forever by Hurricane Katrina. In the weeks leading up to the devastating storm, many people took the advice of the authorities and evacuated. Zack's estranged wife, Lana, asked him to leave New Orleans with her and their children, but he refused. Zack and Addie decided to join the small band of "die-hards" in the French Quarter to ride out the storm. Zack moved into Addie's apartment just before Katrina's arrival, fortified with plenty of drugs and alcohol. When Katrina finally left New Orleans, Zack, Addie and a few others found themselves having to get by without running water, electricity or heat. The resourceful couple found that they could "make do" by salvaging as much alcohol as they could carry from abandoned bars. They spent much of their time sitting on the stoop of their apartment above the Voodoo Temple at 826 North Rampart Street, mixing cocktails that they traded for food and water.

It soon became apparent to their friends and neighbors that their live-in

Zack Bowen, who developed PTSD in Iraq, weathered out Hurricane Katrina by trading cocktails for food and water. *Gracen Deerman.*

Addie Hall's romantic relationship with Zack Bowen was irreparably damaged through the couple's drug abuse and binge drinking. *Gracen Deerman.*

arrangement was far from idyllic. They got used to the sounds of yelling and screaming coming from the open windows of Zack and Addie's apartment. Undoubtedly, their arguments were fueled by their constant drug use and binge drinking. Initially, the lease was in both Addie's and Zack's names because Zack had agreed to pay the first two months' rent in advance. However, after Zack paid the rent on October 4, 2006, Addie asked the landlord to put the lease in her name only. That same night, she kicked him out of her apartment, probably because she had caught him cheating on her.

On October 5, 2006, at 1:00 a.m., Zack strangled Addie to death following a heated argument. He then fell asleep next to her corpse. The next morning, he got dressed, left Addie's decomposing body in the apartment and walked over to the bar, where he began working again. Over the next few days, he set about disposing of his lover's body. He began by carrying it over to the bathtub and dismembering it with a knife and hacksaw. He then placed the pieces in pots and stored them in the refrigerator, the stove and the oven. His increasingly strange behavior alerted his friends, who began asking him about Addie's whereabouts. He simply responded that she had gone back to her family's home in North Carolina. The friends who were aware of Addie's bipolar disorder were surprised by Addie's seemingly impulsive disappearance.

When the reality of what he had done to the woman he loved finally hit home, Zack decided to end it all. He quit his job and devoted the next few weeks to spending his remaining $1,500 on booze, drugs and sex workers. When his money was gone and he was unable to smother the nagging guilt that had been haunting him since Addie's murder, Zack began abusing himself physically. In the suicide note he left behind, Zack admitted to burning himself with cigarettes, one for every year he had been a failure. Security footage taken on October 17, 2006, at 8:30 p.m. showed Zack walking over to the edge of the Omni Hotel Terrace several times and stopping. Finally, he took a final drink, ran to the edge of the terrace and jumped off the roof. The coroner determined that the twenty-eight bruises on his body were probably self-inflicted.

The investigators who entered Zack and Addie's apartment were horrified by what they found. As soon as they walked in the door, they were overcome by a wave of cold air. On the walls were spray-painted phrases like "I'm a failure" and instructions to call Zack's ex-wife and tell her that he loved her. One of these painted messages instructed the police to go the kitchen. There were two pots on the stove. One contained Addie's head; her hands were in the second pot. Her arms and legs were coated in

Zack Bowen murdered and dismembered Addie Hall in their second-floor apartment on rampart street. *Gracen Deerman.*

what appeared to be seasoning. Inside the refrigerator was Addie's torso, wrapped in plastic. On the counter were chopped carrots, which led the police to conclude that Zack was planning to cook them with Addie's limbs. However, an autopsy of Zack's body revealed the total absence of partially digested human body parts.

The sensationalistic nature of Zack's and Addie's deaths was covered in the local and the national media. The couple's grisly end was featured on true crime shows on television. After the Voodoo Spiritual Temple moved out of the apartment building, tours were given of Zack and Addie's apartment for a while. Today, their tragic story stands as a reminder of the negative consequences that can ensue if mental illness is left untreated.

BIBLIOGRAPHY

Books

Blumenthal, Karen. *Bonnie and Clyde: The Making of a Legend*. New York: Viking Press, 2018.

Cassady, Charles, Jr. *Crescent City Crimes*. Atglen, PA: Schiffer, 2017.

Cimino, Al. *True Crime Stories*. London: Arturus, 2019.

Davis, John H. *Mafia Kingfish: Carlos Marcello and the Assassination of John F. Kennedy*. New York: Signet, 1989.

Davis, William C. *The Pirates Laffite: The Treacherous World of the Corsairs of the Gulf*. New York: Harcourt Press, 2005.

Guinn, Jeff. *Go Down Together: The True, Untold Story of Bonnie and Clyde*. New York: Simon & Schuster, 2010.

Lane, Bryan, and Wilfred Gregg. *The Encyclopedia of Mass Murder*. Caldwell, ID: Caxton, 1994.

Oliphant, Ashley, and Beth Yarbrough. *Jean Laffite Revealed: Unraveling One of America's Longest-Running Mysteries*. Lafayette: University of Louisiana Press, 2021.

Pena, Christopher G. *The Strange Case of Dr. Etienne Deschamps*. Gretna, LA: Pelican, 2017.

Rappeley, Charles. *All American Mafiosi*. New York: Doubleday, 1991.

Sifakis, Carl. *The Encyclopedia of American Crime*. New York: Facts on File, 2001.

Taylor, Troy. *Wicked New Orleans*. Charleston, SC: The History Press, 2010.

Time-Life Books. *Mass Murderers*. New York: Time Life Education, 1993.

Williamson, Joel. *The Crucible of Race: Black-White Relations in the American South Since Emancipation*. New York: Oxford University Press, 1984.

Articles

Acadiana Historical. "Midnight Axe Murders: The Killings of Clementine Barnabet." https://acadianahistorical.org/items/show/73.

All That's Interesting. "Derrick Todd Lee, the Baton Rouge Serial Killer Who Tricked His Victims into Letting Him Inside Their Homes." https://allthatsinteresting.com/derrick-todd-lee.

American Battlefield Trust. "Benjamin Butler." https://www.battlefields.org/learn/biographies/benjamin-f-butler.

———. "Pirates in Colonial America." https://www.battlefields.org/learn/articles/pirates-colonial-america.

Beauregard News. "Toni Jo Henry: A Shocking Anniversary." https://www.beauregardnews.com/news/toni-jo-henry-a-shocking-anniversary/.

BlackPast. "Robert Charles Riots (1900)." https://www.blackpast.org/african-american-history/robert-charles-riots-1900/.

CapitalPunishmentUK.org. "Toni Jo Henry, a Love Worth Dying For?" http://www.capitalpunishmentuk.org/tonijo.html.

The Coastal Wanderer. "The Pirate Jean Lafitte." https://coastalwanderer.net/the-pirate-jean-lafitte.

Country Roads. "The Bonnie & Clyde Ambush Museum." https://countryroadsmagazine.com/travel/getaways/bonnie-clyde-ambush-museum/.

———. "One Man, One Gun, One Bullet?" https://www.countryroadsmagazine.com/art-and-culture/history/one-man-one-gun-one-bullet.

CrimeFeed. "Ronald Dominique: 'The Bayou Serial Killer' Who Decimated Gay Louisiana." https://www.investigationdiscovery.com/crimefeed/serial-killer/ronald-dominique-the-bayou-serial-killer-who-decimated-gay-louisiana.

CrimeScribe. "On This Day in 1942—Toni Jo Henry, Louisiana's First (And Only) Woman to Be Electrocuted." https://crimescribe.com/2022/11/28/on-this-day-in-1942-toni-jo-henry-louisianas-first-and-only-woman-to-be-electrocuted.

Criminal Minds Wiki. "Russell Ellwood." https://criminalminds.fandom.com/wiki/Russell_Ellwood.

———. "Sean Vincent Gillis." https://criminalminds.fandom.com/wiki/Sean_Vincent_Gillis.

Deadly Women Wiki. "Antoinette Frank." https://deadlywomen.fandom.com/wiki/Antoinette_Frank.

Facebook. "The Axeman of New Orleans." https://www.facebook.com/axemanofneworleans/.

FBI. "Bonnie and Clyde." https://www.fbi.gov/history/famous-cases/bonnie-and-clyde.

GenealogyBank. "Violent End to Bonnie and Clyde's Life of Crime." https://blog.genealogybank.com/violent-end-to-bonnie-and-clydes-life-of-crime.html.

Ghost City Tours. "The Axeman Murders of New Orleans." https://ghostcitytours.com/new-orleans/ghost-stories/axeman-new-orleans/.

———. "The Haunted Beauregard-Keyes House." https://ghostcitytours.com/new-orleans/hanted-places/beauregard-keyes-house/.

———. "The Story of Zack and Addie." https://ghostcitytours.com/new-Orleans/ghost-stories/zack-addie.

Grunge. "What You Didn't Know about Serial Killer Clementine Barnabet." https://www.grunge.com/365510/what-you-didnt-know-about-serial-killer-clementine-barnabet.

History. "Police Kill Famous Outlaws Bonnie and Clyde." https://www.history.com/this-day-in-history/police-kill-famous-outlaws-bonnie-and-clyde.

"How Madame La Laurie Turned Her New Orleans Mansion into a House of Horrors." Episode of *Yesterday Is History*. Aired December 13, 2021.

Huey Long. "Huey Long: The Man, His Mission, and His Legacy." https://www.hueylong.com/life-times/assassination.php.

IMDb. "Sort by Popularity—Most Popular Movies and TV Shows Tagged with Keyword 'Bonnie and Clyde.'" https://IMDB.com/search/title?title=bonnie.

JSTOR. "The Louisiana-Texas Lumber War of 1911–1912." https://www.jstor.org/stable/4231438.

Justia. "*State v. Code*." https://law.justia.com/cases/Louisiana/supreme-court/1993/91-ka-0998-2.html.

Lafitte's Blacksmith Shop Bar. https://lafittesblacksmithshop.com/Homepage.html.

LA GenWeb Project. "'Leather Britches' Smith and the Grabow Riot." https://lagenweb.org/calcasieu/block/leatherbritches.html.

Legends of America. "Delphine LaLaurie and Her Haunted Mansion in New Orleans." https://www.legendsofamerica.com/lalaurie-mansion/.

———. "Eugene Bunch—A Gentlemanly Train Robber." legendsofamerica. com/eugene-bunch/.

The Line-Up. "Clementine Barnabet and the Church of Sacrifice." https:// the-line-up.com/clementine-barnabet.

Louisiana Myths and Legends. "'Leather Britches' Smith." https:// louisianamythsandlegends.com/leather-britches-smith.

Medium. "The Gruesome Murder-Suicide of the Couple That Peaked During Hurricane Katrina." https://nicolekenney.medium.com/the-gruesome-murder-suicide-of-the-couple-that-peaked-during-hurricane-katrina-6802cff46eb6.

———. "The Gruesome Tale of Zack Bowen and Addie Hall—And What It Says about Our Fascination with True Crime." https://delanirbartlette. medium.com/the-gruesome-tale-of-Zac-bowen-and-addie-hall-and-what-it-says-about-our-fascination-with-true-5c617ObOf6.

Military History. "Mark Essex." https://military-history.fandom.com/wiki/ Mark_Essex.

Mob Museum. "Big Mob Trouble in the Big Easy." https://themobmuseum. org/blog/big-mob-trouble-in-the-big-easy/.

Movieweb. "Every Bonnie and Clyde Movie, Ranked." https://movieweb. com/bonnie-and-clyde-movies.

Murderpedia. "Anne Gates." https://murderpedia.org/female.G/g/gates-anne.htm.

———. "Antoinette Frank." https://murderpedia.org/female.F/f/frank-antoinette.htm.

———. "Mark James Robert Essex." https://murderpedia.org/male.E/e/ essex-mark.htm.

———. "Mary Jane Jackson." https://murderpedia.org/female.J/j/ jackson-mary-jane.htm.

———. "Nathaniel Code." https://murderpedia.org/male.C/c/code-nathaniel.htm.

———. "Ronald Joseph Dominique." https://murderpedia.org/male.D/d/ Dominique-ronald.htm.

———. "Russell Ellwood." https://murderpedia.org/male.E/e/ellwood-russell.htm.

———. "Toni Jo Henry." https://murderpedia.org/female.H/h/henry-toni-jo.htm.

Mustafa, Susan D. "Victims." http://susanmustafa.com/sean-gillis-victims/.

National Park Service. "Jean Lafitte National Historical Park and Preserve Louisiana." https://nps.gov/jela/index.htm.

New Orleans Historical. "The People of Gallatin Street." https://neworleanshistorical.org/items/show/827.

Nola.com. "The Seamy Tale of the Italian Mafia, Extortion and a 1908 Bloody Showdown at the Beauregard-Keyes House." https://www.nola.com/entertainment_life/the-seamy-tale-of-the-italian-mafia-extortion-and-a-1908-bloody-showdown-at-the/article_7ce3276e-bc1a-11eb-bbc5-cb1f9ff6734c.html.

Oxygen True Crime. "'Eyelids Had Been Removed': Serial Killer Strangled Women Then Mutilated Them." https://www.oxygen.com/mark-of-a-serial-killer/crime-news/serial-killer-sean-vincent-gillis-strangled-women.

Paper Monuments. "Robert Charles Riots." https://www.papermonuments.org/pmev-012-robert-charles-riots.

Pelican State of Mind. "Jean Lafitte: Mystery of the Unfound Treasure." https://pelicanstateofmind.com/lousiana-love/jean-lafitte/.

Shiloh to Canaan. "A Train Robbin' Bunch." https://shilohtocanaan.com/2019/01/13/a-train-robbin-bunch/.

64 Parishes. "Huey P. Long, Jr." https://64parishes.org/entry/huey-p-long-jr.

Smithsonian. "The Axeman of New Orleans Preyed on Italian Immigrants." https://www.smithsonianmag.com/history/axeman-new-orleans-preyed-italian-immigrants-180968037.

Social Security History. "Every Man a King." https://www.ssa.gov/history/hlong1.html.

Treasure Net. "School Teacher Turned Bandit." https://treasurenet.com/threads/school-teacher-turned-bandit.127757/.

Tumblr. "Zach Bowen and Addie Hall Crime Case." https://tumblr.com/motherslittlemonster/84871511847/zac-bowen-and-addie-hall-crime-case.

Vox. "'Queen and Slim' Is More Than a Black Version of Bonnie and Clyde." https://vox.com/culture/2019/11/27/20984281/queen-slim-review-bonnie-clyde.

Where Y'at. "The Tragic Tale of Zach & Addie." https://whereyat.com/the-tragedy-of-zach-addie.

World History Encyclopedia. "Jean Lafitte." https://worldhistory.org/jean-Lafitte/.

WSDU. "Rogers LaCaze, Antoinette Frank's Co-Conspirator, No Longer Facing Execution after Sentencing." https://www.wdsu.com/article/rogers-lacaze-antoinette-franks-co-conspirator-no-longer-on-death-row-after-resentencing/30222316.

Magazines

Dolgin, Daniel. "The Bonnie & Clyde Ambush Museum." *Country Roads Magazine.* September 25, 2020.

Turner-Neal, Chris. "Oh My Darling, Clementine: Nineteen Murders, a Death Cult, and a Wild Confession." *Country Roads Magazine.* September 22, 2022.

Newspapers

Associated Press. "Woman Accused of Murdering Estranged Husband." December 20, 1987.

Bath, Alison. "Sentence Ended Murder Spree but Not Killer's Life." *Shreveport Times*, November 3, 2015.

———. "Young Mother May Have Been Code's First Victim." *Town Talk*, August 17, 2015.

Chicago Tribune. "Woman Serving Time in Death of Spouse Inherits $25,000." May 26, 1992.

DeRobertis, Jacqueline. "Dr. Carl Weiss Jr., Who Questioned Whether His Father Assassinated Huey Long, Dies at 84." *Advocate*, August 2, 2019.

Lake Charles Echo. "Bunch Killed." August 26, 1892.

Morris, David. "Middle-Aged Clerk Turns to Robbing Trains." *Copper Cove Leader Press*, August 8, 2017.

ABOUT THE AUTHOR

Photograph courtesy of Marilyn Brown.

Dr. Alan Brown is a professor of English and folklore at the University of West Alabama. His research interests include ghost lore, urban legends and true crime. When he is not taking trips with his wife, Marilyn, Dr. Brown is playing and studying with his three grandsons: Cade Walker, Owen Walker and Samuel Reynolds. He also enjoys watching vintage movies and television shows with his wife and their Maltese, Holly.